ISBN 978-1-331-24439-4
PIBN 10163531

1 MONTH OF
FREE
READING

at
www.ForgottenBooks.com

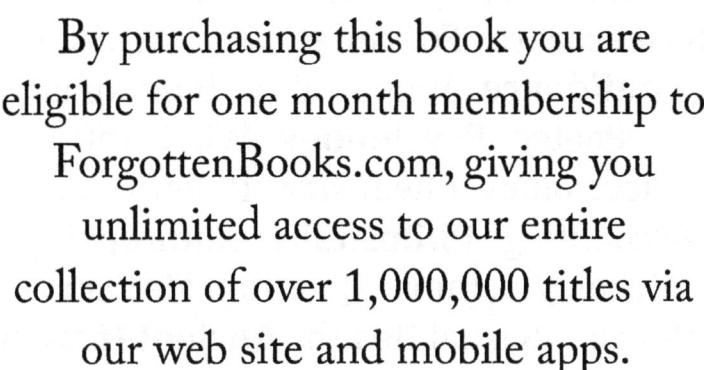

By purchasing this book you are eligible for one month membership to ForgottenBooks.com, giving you unlimited access to our entire collection of over 1,000,000 titles via our web site and mobile apps.

To claim your free month visit:
www.forgottenbooks.com/free163531

MY DIARY IN MEXICO

IN 1867, INCLUDING THE

LAST DAYS OF THE EMPEROR MAXIMILIAN;

WITH LEAVES FROM

THE DIARY OF THE PRINCESS SALM-SALM,

ETC.

BY FELIX SALM-SALM,

GENERAL, FIRST AIDE-DE-CAMP, AND CHIEF OF THE HOUSEHOLD
OF HIS LATE MAJESTY THE EMPEROR MAXIMILIAN
OF MEXICO.

IN TWO VOLUMES.

VOL. I.

LONDON:
RICHARD BENTLEY, NEW BURLINGTON STREET,
Publisher in ordinary to Her Majesty.
1868.

F. BENTLEY AND CO., PRINTERS, SHOE LANE, FLEET STREET, LONDON.

PREFACE.

In the codicil to the last Will of Emperor Maximilian of Mexico occurs the following passage :—

" § 15. I will that an historical account of the three years of my sojourn in Mexico and the preparatory period shall be written, with the assistance of those documents which are kept in England and Miramar.

" I desire that the ex-minister Don Fern. Ramirez and Prince Filipp de Salm-Salm would have the kindness to undertake this work."

Although I knew of the fact that my person was mentioned in several places of the Emperor's last Will, I only became certain of it by one of the witnesses who had signed it. Neither the contents of that last Will, nor even the dispositions referring to my person, were communicated to me; and I tried in vain, in Vienna and elsewhere, to obtain a copy of it. At last I thought it best to apply for further information to the First Lord Steward of His Majesty the Emperor of Austria, General Prince Constantin von Hohenlohe, and to request his highness to indicate by what means I could get access to the documents, which I should require to fulfil the desire of the Emperor Maximilian, as expressed in his last Will, and of which I had been informed by chance.

In reply to my letter of the 22nd of July, 1868, I received from the prince the following letter, dated July 29th:—

VIENNA, *July 29th*, 1868.

YOUR HIGHNESS,—I beg to reply to your highness' agreeable letter of the 22nd instant, that His late Majesty the Emperor Maximilian indeed expressed in his last Will a desire, that the history of the last years of his government in Mexico might be written by your highness and the ex-minister Don Fernando Ramirez.

As, however, the publication of the last Will of His late Majesty only took place in the office of the Lord Steward of the Household, and the execution of the arrangements in reference to this last Will belong to the province of the office of the Lord Marshal, I thought it right to send your highness' letter to the Lord Marshal, Count Kuefstein, for further consideration.

At the same time, I avail myself of this opportunity to renew to your highness the. expression of my perfect regard.

HOHENLOHE.

To his highness Prince Felix de Salm-Salm, etc.,
Castle Anholt.

P.S. As this letter had been returned by the post as not to be delivered, I beg to send it now to the address of the Counsellor-at-Law Rump in Bocholt, who has been named to me as your highness' attorney-general; and at the same time I beg to enclose a copy of the reply, which I received in the meantime from the Lord-Marshal, Count Kuefstein.

(By order) A. JMHOE,

J. R. Counsellor at Court.

The letter mentioned in that postscriptum is the following :—

VIENNA, *August 4th*, 1868.

In answering your highness' kind note of the 22nd of July, 1868, I have the honour to reply :—

The assertion made in the letter herewith

returned of Prince Salm is correct; for § 15 of the codicil of his late Majesty Maximilian of Mexico (which though not signed was ordered to be published by his Majesty the Emperor, our most gracious Lord) reads as follows :—

"I will that an historical account of the three years of my sojourn in Mexico, and the preparatory period shàll be written with the assistance of those documents kept in England and Miramar.

"I desire that the ex-minister Don Fern. Ramirez and Prince Filipp de Salm-Salm would have the kindness to undertake this work."

In consequence of this, the request of Prince Salm to permit him an insight into the respective documents is *sufficiently founded*, but the granting of this request depends upon the will of His Majesty; as, according to § 29 of the statutes of the Imperial house, no publication or execution of a last Will can be made without the consent of the chief of the Most Illustrious Imperial house. As His Majesty by an autograph note of September 10, 1867, ordered the publication of the last Will of his brother, of April 5, 1864, " *with the omission of the direction contained in that last Will, in reference to the nomination of an executor of that last Will,*" it is possible that his Majesty might have some just objection against an inspection *of at least all* confidential state documents referring to the three years *régent epoque* and the preparatory period. It seems therefore doubtless that the Will of His Majesty in this respect was, by all means, to be ascertained.

But it is not within the competency of the Lord Marshal's Office to request it, for the documents which could be meant in this case, have never been in the hands of this office, and are by no means an object for its transactions, and to this the ministry of this office is limited. KUEFSTEIN.

To his highness the I. Royal,
Major-General Prince Constantin von Hohenlohe,
First Lord Steward of His Majesty.

The love alone which I preserve in my heart for the memory of my unfortunate Emperor, would make it a sacred duty for me to fulfil, to the best of my ability, every desire expressed by him in his last Will; but his desire is still increased by my knowing how anxious he was to be judged justly by posterity. This, however, is only possible with the knowledge of all circumstances, which cannot possibly be acquired so long as certain transactions remain a secret, and the documents referring to them are kept by persons who have a particular interest in preventing their publication.

The Emperor held these documents in very high estimation, and feeling that his position in Mexico was rather precarious at the time when the Empress left for Europe, and when he was surrounded by traitors, he did not think these documents safe enough in Mexico, and confided them to the Empress to keep them safely in Europe.

I have no certain knowledge about the contents of these papers; but I know how uneasy Maximilian felt about them, when he received the news of the illness of his consort, and that he asked me most urgently to get possession of them, if required, " even revolver in hand," and to write by the use of them, the history of his government.

In the last Will of the Emperor it is stated, that these documents were in England and in Miramar, but a great personage to whom I wrote on that subject, answered in reference to the documents, and especially the correspondence between the Emperor of the French and Marshal Bazaine : " On dit aujourd'hui que le Pape en est le dépositaire."

It is most likely that different parts of
those documents are in England, Miramar, and
Rome; but I had only a certainty about those in
Miramar, for which reason I began to take
steps in that direction; with what success may
be seen from the above letters.

I do not know yet upon what further measures I shall decide, but I believe I am justified
in my hope that His Majesty the Emperor of
Austria will readily support my efforts in vindi-
cating the memory of his brother.

I do not know who is the keeper of the
documents in England. It is said that they
are in the hands of Her Majesty the Queen;
but before I have more certain information
I do not think it proper to obtrude on a mere
" on dit," either His Holiness the Pope, or
Her Majesty the Queen of England.

As soon as I shall be placed in a position
to satisfy the desire of the late Emperor,
I shall enter into communication with Don
Fernando Ramirez, to fulfil together with him,
and as well as I can, the last Will of our beloved late Emperor.

Supposing that it would be desirable to the
Imperial family of Austria to receive as soon as
possible an authentic account of the last months

of the Emperor, I wrote, when still in prison in Querétaro, a narrative of them, and forwarded it to the Secretary of State, Baron Beust, in Vienna. To this I did not receive an answer, and when I had the honour afterwards of an audience with His Majesty the Emperor, he did not mention anything about it either.

As probably a considerable time will elapse before I shall be in a position to write the history of the government of the Emperor Maximilian, and as I have received from many sides the intimation that a publication about the occurrences in Querétaro was expected from me, I resolved to publish such a narrative, with the assistance of my diary.

This would have been done perhaps sooner, if I had not been detained a prisoner in Mexico until November 13, 1867, and after my arrival in Europe, had I not had to wait several months for the arrival of my effects and papers.

As to these papers, I am sorry to say, that a good many of them have been lost, partly during the occupation of Querétaro by the Liberals, and partly during my imprisonment. I regret especially the loss of those contained in a small trunk, which I confided to a Liberal officer when I was suddenly transferred from one prison to another. When I got the trunk again, all the papers had disappeared, though a sum of money had not been touched.

I beg to remind the reader that it is by no means my intention now to write a "history," of the last months of the Mexican Empire, but only to give a narrative of my personal experiences. The following pages make no other pretensions than to be faithful to truth.

Relative to this truthfulness I refer to the evidence of General and ex-Secretary of War, Don Severo de Castillo, my esteemed friend and companion in sorrow, as also to my other friend and fellow-sufferer, General Escobar, men of high honour, and held in respect by every one. These gentlemen, who for a long time lived with me in the same prison cell, gave me many explanations about things of which I had only an imperfect knowledge, and completed my narrative of the well-known facts by giving me authentic details.

In regard to my judgments about persons who played a part in the events which occurred in the tragedy of Querétaro, I must say that they are generally the result of an exchange of ideas between the late Emperor and myself.

As my wife took an active part in many of

the events related in the following pages, I requested her to add her narrative with mine.

Though more than a year has elapsed since the death of the Emperor Maximilian, and the interest of the public in this tragedy may have become somewhat weakened; and though others may have anticipated me in some particulars, still I hope that this true, simple narrative of an eye-witness will not be thought superfluous.

FELIX SALM-SALM.

RORSCHACK, ON THE LAKE OF CONSTANCE,
September, 1868.

CONTENTS.

CONTENTS

DIARY OF PRINCE SALM-SALM.

MARCH TO QUERETARO.

DURING the great civil war in North America, I
served the United States from 1861 to the close
of it, first as Colonel and Chief of the General
Staff of the German Division, then as commander of a regiment, and later as Brigadier-
General and civil and military Governor of
North Georgia, under J. B. Steedman, commanding division.

After the war I was recommended by
twenty-six Senators for a position in the U. S.
regular army; but I never felt at home in that
country, and was horrified at the idea of living
a dreary and idle life in some little garrison
beyond the pale of civilization. I had been a
soldier from my early youth; and, having been
educated in the Cadet-house of Berlin, became
an officer when still very young, and saw active

1

service in the Holstein war, for which I was decorated, and received besides from the King of Prussia a sword of honour, with the words " Fuer Tapferkeit " engraved on it.

To speak the truth, I was a soldier with all my soul, and war was my element. What I had seen of it in Europe and America served only to make me more eager to extend my experience; and I resolved to offer my services to the Emperor Maximilian of Mexico, for whose person and civilizing task I had always felt great sympathy.

As I was not personally known to the Emperor, I had to provide myself with testimonials in reference to my military ability, and with letters of recommendation from influential persons. The former I got with the most friendly readiness from the President of the United States and the generals under whom I had made the campaign; and letters of recommendation were given to me by the Prussian minister in Washington, Baron Gerolt, the French minister, Marquis de Montholon, and the Austrian minister, Baron de Wydenbruck, who kindly wrote a letter to the Emperor Maximilian, to be delivered to him oy Count Thun, the Austrian minister in Mexico.

Thus prepared, as I imagined, quite sufficiently, I embarked for Mexico from New York,

February 20th, 1866, accompanied by Captain Baron von Groeben, a distant relative of mine, who had been my aide-de-camp in the U. S. wars.

On my arrival in Mexico the Emperor was not there; but I applied, by letter, for a position in the army, and was assured by the Imperial Secretary of the Cabinet, Mr. Pierron, that the Emperor was very much inclined to grant my request, but that my appointment was delayed by the efforts of Count Thun, who retained even the letter which he had received for the Emperor. When the Prussian minister in Mexico, Baron von Magnus, asked him for the reason of his opposition against me, he answered, " The prince has been recommended as Prince Eugene of Savoy : could not have been better ; but it is against my principles to recommend him." To his efforts, and those of General Count Thun, his relative, who commanded the Austrian corps, it was owing that no Prussian found a position in that army.

When, later, I was invited, together with Baron Magnus, to dine with the Emperor, Maximilian told the Baron that many intrigues had been practised to prevent my appointment, and that it had been even said I was not Prince Salm, but an impostor.

The kindness and exertions of the Prussian

minister succeeded at last, however, in con-
quering all opposition, and on July 1st, 1866,
I was appointed colonel of the general staff
and detailed on the staff of the French General
Negri, who commanded the so-called auxiliary
division, which consisted of one French brigade,
the Austrian and Belgian corps, and the troops
of the city and the valley of Mexico.

As the princess, my wife, intended to follow
me to Mexico as soon as I should have a position in the army, the Emperor gave me leave to
bring her; and I proceeded to Vera Cruz,
where I fell ill with the yellow fever, to which I
nearly became a victim.

The departure of my wife from New York
had been delayed, and when I was on my way
to the United States I met her in Havana, and
returned with her directly to Mexico.

Soon after our arrival one of the ministers
proposed to enter into certain negociations with
the United States' Government about the recog-
nition of the Emperor; and as my wife and
I were well acquainted with the President, the
senators and members of Congress, we were
ordered to go on this mission. For expenses
that might occur, we should take with us two
millions of dollars, in gold, under the superintendence of the Councillor of State, von Herzfeld
or some other higher officer.

Before this affair was arranged, however, the distressing news of the illness of the Empress arrived. The Emperor went to Orizaba, and the whole business was at last dropped, as circumstances materially changed.

An idle life was utterly disgusting to me, and I heartily desired to see active service in the field. I requested the Secretary of War to permit me to accompany, as a volunteer, an expedition of the Belgian corps into the interior.

We marched over Pachuca to Tulancingo, where we relieved a detachment of the Austrian corps, commanded by Lieut.-Colonel Pollack, who was to assist Jalappa, and left, November 12th, at five o'clock a.m. At eleven o'clock a.m., the Liberal General Martinez, with six thousand men, appeared already before Tulancingo.

The city was not fortified, and our troops consisted only of eight hundred men of the Belgian corps and eight hundred Mexicans; and their commander, Colonel Van der Smissen, sent three Indian messengers, with letters hidden in cigarets, to Lieut.-Colonel Pollack, requesting him to return and to assist in attacking the enemy. The gallant colonel consulted his gallant officers, and they gallantly resolved not to follow the invitation.

Too weak to undertake anything against the besiegers, I took care to fortify the place as well as circumstances would permit.

Whilst occupied in this manner, I was informed that Colonel Peralta, who commanded the 6th Mexican regiment of cavalry in the city, was in communication with the enemy. As my proofs were not sufficient to convict him, measures were taken to prevent bad consequences.

I had fortified the palace of the bishop and a church in such a manner as to serve us as a redoubt. The Mexican troops were quartered in the palace, and the Belgians in the church, from which all the fortifications of the palace could be flanked. I had, moreover, laid a mine under the building by a number of competent Belgian sergeants, to blow up the whole concern should the Mexicans prove traitors.

The measures taken by us seemed to impress the enemy, who did not dare to attack us, but who tried to obtain possession of the city in a less dangerous manner.

On December 1st I received, in a mysterious manner, a letter from the Liberal Colonel Brulio C. Picazo, in which I was requested to come alone and unarmed to the hacienda St. Nicola el Grande. He promised me safety on his word of honour, and that he himself would also be there alone without any escort. The time for the appointment was eight o'clock the following morning. After having consulted with Colonel Van der Smissen, I resolved to run the risk of the tempting adventure.

Accordingly, next morning I was on my way to·the hacienda, alone, and armed only with a small revolver in my pocket. When on arriving at the hacienda, I was rather surprised to meet there two videttes; but, passing them without any sign of distrust, they saluted me respectfully.

Colonel Picazo was a very well-educated gentleman, who spoke several languages fluently, and had the manners of a man of the world. He assured me that the cause of the Emperor was a lost one, and, moreover, sketched the whole state of affairs in a manner which was not flattering, but unfortunately was true. Then he endeavoured to induce me to persuade Colonel Van der Smissen to surrender the place, in which case he would pay me twenty thousand piasters.

As I knew that such an offer is thought a matter of common occurrence in Mexico, and that no offence was intended, I contented myself with simply declining his proposal, on which the colonel told me that if we did not surrender within five days,, we should be attacked with ten thousand men. I answered that we should be happy to receive them. The whole affair was discussed over a cigar and a glass of brandy.

When leaving, the colonel accompanied me to the yard, shook hands with me, and I returned to the city, glad to escape thus, as I had seen in the hacienda a detachment of thirty horse.

We had, however, no opportunity of showing our courage on this occasion; for at the close of December we received the order from Marshal Bazaine to surrender Tulancingo to General Martinez.

The chief of the staff of this general, Colonel Cruz, came on the 27th under a flag of truce, to arrange about the surrender. I saw in his hand the same order which we had received, and signed, in the name of Bazaine, by Colonel Bover, chief of staff of the French expeditionary army. Colonel Cruz made no secret of it, that they had been on the best understanding with the French, and that as to this retreat, they kept purposely out of the way.

The troops of General Martinez advanced the same evening close to our works.

We were also informed that a noted guerilla chief, of the name of Carebajal, had arrived with a band of eight hundred men, from Uacinango, and Colonel Van der Smissen gave orders that no officer or man should go outside the barricades. Captain Timerance, of the Belgian corps, who wished to say "good-bye" to a lady friend outside, passed the barricades at ten o'clock p.m., was attacked and wounded by Carebajal's guerillas and taken prisoner. On being requested to send back the officer, Carebajal answered that he would do so if we would first let him enter the city; but Van der Smissen told him to keep the disobedient captain, who was, however, released later, at the request of the Spanish consul, and sent to Mexico.

At seven o'clock in the evening Colonel Peralta, previously mentioned, appeared at the lodging of Colonel Van der Smissen, for orders in reference to the marching next morning. His unusually nervous manner was noticed by everyone present, and when he left, Colonel Van der Smissen said to me: "You will see that he will go over to the enemy; but I shall be prepared for it."

Peralta had been ordered to form with his cavalry the advance guard, and one company of the Belgian corps was now ordered to follow him closely, and its captain was instructed to fire upon the Mexicans as soon as they should attempt to go over to the enemy.

At six o'clock next morning the Belgian corps and the Mexican infantry, under Colonel Campos, a true and reliable officer, stood ready in the market-place, when we suddenly saw coming, in full gallop, with drawn sword, First Lieutenant Goslich, the only German officer serving in the 6th Mexican cavalry. Colonel Peralta, who had ordered his regiment to be ready at four o'clock a.m., requested Lieutenant Goslich to come to his side, and he then informed him that he intended to go over with his regiment to the Liberals, and that he might consider himself a prisoner. The lieutenant was silent, as he could do nothing; but when after a time the colonel turned aside to speak to some other officer, he drew his sword, set spurs to his horse, and, brandishing his blade over his head, succeeded in passing unharmed through the whole regiment, and arrived safely in the market-place.

Peralta was, however, not the only cur who deserted: another far more valuable dog, Jimmy, the pet of my wife, was missing. My wife had accompanied me in all my campaigns in North America, and frequently shared my tent for months. She had joined me in Mexico, and of course her Jimmy also, as he had never left her during the whole war in America. But instead of becoming used to warlike noise, he had brought home from it the most intense aversion against any sound resembling gun-shots or drums. When he, therefore, arrived at the market-place, and heard the drums and saw so many shooting engines, he popped off to our old quarters at the Spanish vice-consul's, Mr. Gayon, and no servant being thought worthy to touch his precious skin, my tyrant insisted on my going myself.

When I—the rather long-legged favourite under my arm—stepped out of the house, I was not very agreeably surprised on seeing before me an officer of the enemy with five men, who, according to agreement, ought to have entered the city only at the moment when we left it. However, nothing happened; the men of the enemy saluted, and I joined my troops.

Half an hour after we left Tulancingo our rearguard was attacked by Carebajal's robbers, who retired, however, after having lost a few dead.

In Tulancingo the Belgian corps had already received the order by which it was disbanded, and at the same time the offer of Marshal Bazaine to provide for the passage of the men to Europe, which was gladly accepted by most of them. When we came to Buena Vista, which is on the road between Puebla and Mexico, orders came to stop there until further notice.

On the evening of January 2nd, 1867, we were informed that the Emperor would pass

the place on his way from Orizaba to Mexico,
next morning, and we were of course ready to
receive him.

The Emperor drove in a little carriage with
four white mules, and was accompanied by
an escort of the lancers and hussars of the
Austrian corps, which was going to be disbanded in Mexico, and also by a detachment of
French Zouaves on horseback. With the Emperor were General Marquez and his staff,
Colonel Schaffer, Colonel Lamadrid, Captain
Von Gröller, of the Austrian frigate "Elisa-
beth," Father Fischer, and Dr. Basch, his
physician.

General Don Leonardo Marquez is a little,
lively man, with black hair and black, keen eyes.
He wears a full beard, to hide a disfiguring
scar on his cheek from a bullet-wound. His
atrocious cruelty has won for him the name of
the "Alva of Mexico," which he richly deserves. As an old chief of the Church
party, he was very intimate with all the
priests. Though an extremely brave soldier,
he was but a very indifferent general, as he
had no idea whatever of strategical movements. His most valuable talent was that of
organizing troops.

Colonel Lamadrid, a very able and amiable
officer, who commanded a regiment of Cazadores

a caballo, was killed a week later on an expedition to Cuernavaca.

Colonel Schaffer had served formerly in the Austrian navy, under the Emperor, when still high admiral, and was very intimate with him. He was always near him.

Father Augustine Fischer is a tall, portly gentleman, very intelligent, and just as ambitious. He had been appointed only a few days ago " Cabinet-Secretary " of the Emperor, and was in citizen dress. About his morals very queer reports were in circulation, and it was well known that he, though a priest, had many children in different parts of the country.

When the Emperor, after the news of the distressing state of the Empress, went to Orizaba, and the French and Americans expected every moment his abdication, Marquez, Miramon, and Father Fischer, followed him to that place, and succeeded in persuading him to stay.

Marquez and Miramon promised that the Church party would assist him sufficiently with troops and money, if he would only rely entirely upon his Mexican subjects, and were very free with their word of honour.

The Emperor knew very well the unreliable character of such promises, and would, perhaps, not have been induced by them to stay, had not

Father Fischer, who well knew his noble and self-sacrificing character, painted in the darkest colours the future condition of his friends in Mexico, after his departure from the country.

The Emperor therefore resolved not to abdicate, to the great consternation of Marshal Bazaine and General Castleneau, who were sent on a special mission by Napoleon III., as it prevented their whole scheme of arranging affairs with the Liberal Government, under General Ortega.

Father Fischer perhaps meant well to the Emperor, but the interests of the Roman Church ranked first in his estimation.

Dr. S. Basch is a little, very intelligent, modest gentleman, and excellent physician, and was very devoted to his master. Later, in Querétaro, he was made also chief physician of all the hospitals, and sacrified himself day and night to his onerous duty.

In the evening the Imperial headquarters were at Ayotla, about fourteen leagues from Mexico. I rode over thither, and after having requested, through Father Fischer, an audience, I received authorization from the Emperor to raise a regiment of cavalry, with European volunteers from the Belgian legion and others.

On the 6th of January the Belgian legion marched over Rio Frio, Puentes Esmalucan, and San Martin to Puebla, where they gave up their rifled battery and their excellent muskets to the French General Douai. I was very much astonished when I found later these identical arms in the hands of the troops of the Liberal General Porfirio Diaz!

The Belgian legion now marched to Vera Cruz, where they embarked for Europe on January 20th, 1867.

I had accompanied the legion to Puebla, in the hope of winning some recruits for my new regiments. In this undertaking I was, however, hindered very much by a circular of Mr. Hooricks, secretary of the Belgian legation, in which the Belgians were warned against attempts to persuade them to remain in Mexico, the Government at home requiring their services.

A similar paper was published by the Austrian *chargé d'affaires*, Baron Lago, and many Austrian officers also did all they could to prevent their countrymen from enlisting.

Seeing that it was impossible for me to raise a regiment, I returned to Mexico, and requested the Emperor, through Father Fischer, to employ me somewhere else in active service. The oily priest promised. I went every day to see him, and he continued his promises, but my affairs did not make any progress at all.

Count Khevenhüller, and Baron Hammerstein, two very brave Austrians, succeeded better in raising troops. Under great difficulties the count organized a regiment of hussars, and the baron a battalion of four or five hundred men.

At last came the 5th of February, the day which was to free Mexico from its tyrannical liberators, the French. It was one of those clear and bright Mexican mornings; all the population was in the streets, and in a pleasant excitement. The departure of the French was a happy event for everybody, for they had made themselves hated by all parties. I need not speak about the behaviour of Marshal Bazaine, it has been appreciated in many publications. He may have acted according to his instructions, but if so he did it not only in his own peculiar brutal manner, but probably overstepped them in many things, as it suited his boundless and rapacious ambition.

The French officers imitated the marshal, and their arrogance and covetousness were intolerable. This Mexican expedition was for them merely an agreeable change, and was preferable to a dreary garrison life in France. It was also a good opportunity of enriching themselves; they did not care a straw either for Maximilian or the alleged humanizing or civilizing inteutions of their Emperor. They despised the

Mexicans with French arrogance, and insulted the inhabitants of the city every day. Gentlemen on the side walks who did not get out of their way fast enough, were kicked from it in the street; and ladies who ventured to go out were insulted by their low importunity. The officers of the Imperial Mexican army preferred to go in citizen's dress, as French officers and soldiers did not return their salute.

Early in the morning already the numerous balconies of Mexico were filled with black-eyed ladies, the *reboso* thrown coquettishly over the head and left shoulder. I stood with my wife on the balcony of the hotel Iturbide, in the calle Francisco, and beside us were Count and Countess Seguier and several ladies of French officers. The French marched at nine o'clock a.m., past the Alameda, through the calle San Francisco and calle Plateros, over the Plaza de Armos, passed the Imperial palace, and left by the Garita San Antonio. At their head marched Marshal Bazaine, followed by a brilliant staff: no friendly word, no farewell, greeted the hated oppressors; the people saw them pass in silence, and the beautiful women looked down from the balconies on the fine and coquettishly turning officers with a contemptuous smile. The Emperor did not go to the window when they passed, but he could not forbear looking from behind the curtain on the soldiers of his treacherous ally.

When the troops passed our hotel the French ladies waved their handkerchiefs and went into ecstacies. "What a brilliant army! with such soldiers the world may be conquered. And that they will do. 'Let them only return to *la belle France,* and they will march against Berlin and take it *à la bayonet!*" I did not regard their talk, but only wished to be in Berlin to meet them there.

The citadel was evacuated only a day later, for the garrison required time to destroy forty guns, together with the ammunition. Six rifled guns and four thousand shells were carefully buried that the Liberals might dig them up again at a later period. This purpose was, however, betrayed, and they fell into the hands of the Imperialists. I am able to affirm that Bazaine offered General Porfirio Diaz to deliver Mexico into his hands, as the general told me so himself in November; but Porfirio Diaz declined, adding that he hoped to be able to take the city himself.

The day after, the people of Mexico were frightened again by the appearance of many French soldiers in the streets. They were, however, only deserters from the French army. In this manner the marshal lost on his way to

Vera Cruz not less than six thousand men, who belonged for the greater part to the Legion étranger. The marshal claimed them, but General Marquez answered that he might come and fetch them himself.

As it was the urgent desire of Napoleon to induce the Emperor Maximilian to abdicate and to return to Europe, the marshal did all he could to compel him to do so by assisting the Liberals. He delivered to them not only many cities and arms, but placed as many impediments as possible in the way of organizing a new army, in which he was aided by the Austrian and Belgian ministers.

Thus the Emperor was, after the departure of the French, in a very precarious position; but Marquez did all he could to make good his word, at least, so far as to exert himself to the utmost in organizing new troops, whilst Father Fischer poured soothing words into Maximilian's ear, and the cabinet promised golden impossibilities.

About the plans of the Emperor nothing was known, but on the evening of the 12th of February, a report ran through Mexico that he would place himself at the head of all disposable troops, and leave Mexico next morning, to join Miramon in Querétaro, where also the Generals Castillo and Mendez were expected to be. With their combined troops it was his purpose to endeavour to prevent the concentration of the enemy in the north, and its advance against Mexico.

As soon as I heard of it, I went to see Baron Magnus, who confirmed the report, and I asked him to support my request to be ' permitted to accompany the Emperor. He was ready to do so, but he did not succeed. My request was refused, as the Emperor had promised to leave.all foreigners behind, and to rely exclusively on his Mexican subjects. Marquez and his comrades feared the influence of the Germans on the Emperor, and perhaps still more their superior knowledge in the science of war.

When I was awakened on the following morning by the well-known noise in the streets preceding the marching of troops, I went out, and soon became convinced that all foreigners had been indeed left behind—even the only rifled battery which the army possessed.

The Emperor joined his troops outside the garita at six o'clock a.m., and commenced his march to Querétaro. On his way to the next halting-place (Feb. 13th, 1867) he was attacked by the guerilla bands of Forgoza, who were, however, soon beaten off.

It seemed to me against nature that I should not accompany the Emperor on his expedition, and I was very unhappy. As early as was convenient, I went again to see Baron Magnus, hoping to find some consolation. On this occasion I was not disappointed. The minister told me that General Don Saniago Vidaurri was to join the Emperor at his first halting-place (Quicliclan), and that he would, perhaps, consent to take me with him. I thereupon hastened to see the general, who promised to attach me to his staff, if I could procure an authorization to that purpose from the Secretary of War.

With that answer I returned to Baron Magnus, who ordered his carriage to drive me to the secretary. But the coachman unluckily managed to run a wheel against a corner post, and in some manner or other the pole broke. We did not pay any attention to this bad omen, but continued our way on foot. The Secretary of War gave the required order with more readiness than we expected, and by one o'clock p.m., I reported myself at the quarters of the general.

General Don Saniago Vidaurri was a tall, lank man, of about sixty, who did not look in the least like a Mexican, but resembled, both in his external appearance and manners, a North American. He was, in my opinion, the most remarkable man in all Mexico, Juarez not excepted.

For years he had been one of the principal
chiefs of the Liberal party, and had frequently
fought against Marquez and Miramon. He was
then governor of the State of Nueva Leon, and
the order of this State was the wonder of all
Mexico. The mails went regularly there, and
even money could be sent safely by them without an escort.

General Vidaurri was disgusted with the
anarchical state of Mexico, of which he did not
see the probability of an end. He had, moreover, personal difficulties with Juarez, and pronounced himself in favour of the Emperor Maximilian, of whom he expected, what appeared to
him the most essential thing, the restoration of
a regular government. As he was a very prominent and very popular man, his going over
to the Imperial party had a great influence on ·
the inhabitants of his State, and many respect-
able men and officers followed him. As he did
not pronounce at all for the Church party, but
always remained a Liberal, the party of Marquez
distrusted him, perhaps, and kept him away
from the Emperor. A man, however, of his
influence and talent could not be neglected;
and a few days before the Emperor left, he sent
for Vidaurri. He was to accompany the Emperor to Querétaro, in order to go thence to the
north, where he was so well and favourably

known, there to organize the states politically and military, for which task a better fitted man could not be found anywhere.

The general was also a very good man, and especially kind and amiable towards me, which created at first some jealousy amongst his followers, who looked on me with coldness. An exception should be made by me in favour of a stout German captain, of the name of Willmann, who had been more than twenty years the aide, or rather the "maid of all work," of the general. I saw him even black his boots. He had been originally a watchmaker, and was, I imagine, a Suabian: the broken German in which he conversed with me had, at least, a very strong Suabian twang. He was a very good, little, nervous fellow, who did all he could to assist and serve me. The son of the general, Colonel Don Ignatio Vidaurri, myself, and the factotum-captain, were always with the general.

The general was to be escorted by a detachment of the hussars of Khevenhüller, commanded by Captain Echegaray, and the Lieutenants Pawlowski and Koehlig; and by a detachment of Cavalleros des los Fronteros, for the most part men who followed Vidaurri from the north.

We were to leave Mexico at one o'clock p.m., but our march was delayed until five o'clock, as the Secretary of War could not make up his mind to part with the money which Vidaurri was to take to the Emperor. Aide after aide had to be sent for it. At last it came at half-past four.

To persuade the Emperor to stay, the ministers had been still more extravagant with their promises than even Marquez, Miramon, and Father Fischer. They promised golden mountains, and laid before the Emperor fictitious financial statements, which dazzled him, and which he believed to be true, as he was no great financier. However, all the money the ministers could furnish the Emperor for his campaign were 50,000 miserable pesos!

General Vidaurri drove in a carriage to the garita, where he mounted his horse. He was received by the great crowd in the streets with loud acclamations, which showed the popularity of this distinguished man. On our march we were also attacked by the guerillas, but the hussars drove them off sabre in hand.

When we arrived past midnight at Quicliclan we found all quarters occupied by the troops of the Emperor, and all provisions eaten by them. I encamped with the two German officers of hussars in the yard of a large hacienda, and we were compelled to be satisfied with a supper of " crackers " and cold water.

At six o'clock the following morning the troops were ready for the march. When General Vidaurri saw me, he scolded me in a friendly way because I had not shared his quarters, which I had not done for fear of importuning him.

The Emperor was received by the troops with great enthusiasm. He mounted a very fine piebald horse, with Mexican saddle and bridle, wore the general's coat without epaulets, dark trousers, and over them boots reaching up to his knees, and a large Mexican sombrero. He was armed with a sabre, and two revolvers attached to the saddle. He held always in his hand a single, very simple field-glass (which he gave me later as a keepsake), through which he scanned the country before him very frequently.

As the Emperor rode along the line, General Vidaurri and myself stood on the right wing. On his coming near us he gave his hand to Vidaurri, and on seeing me he smiled, and exclaimed, "Zounds! Salm, how did you come here?"

"Your Majesty would not take me with you," I answered; "and as I would not remain idle in Mexico, I requested General Vidaurri to take me with him."

The Emperor observed: "You know the reasons why I refused your request; however, I am very glad to see you here." With that he shook hands with me in a very friendly way, and rode on.

Our march led us first to Tepeji, and for the first time I had an opportunity of admiring a Mexican order of marching. The intervals between the different troops were very great, and made still greater by their very heavy and extremely badly-teamed artillery, which compelled it to stop every moment. Had we had before us an European enemy, this circumstance might have become fatal, and the more so, as our flanks were not even protected in any other manner than by an army of women and children, who follow every Mexican army, and who, again, are escorted by an army of very ugly, cowardly curs.

How reliable such a Mexican army is may be gathered from the circumstance that the soldiers are all day very carefully guarded by their officers, and are always locked up in haciendas during the night, to prevent them from running away.

The Emperor was accompanied by General Marquez, his quartermaster-general, with his personal staff, which consisted of people without any capacity or ability. The only exception was Major William von Montlong, who served formerly in the Austrian corps, and became the cabinet-officer of the Emperor, and had to act as assistant to the cabinet-secretary.

The chief of the staff of General Marquez was Major Waldemar von Becker, formerly a Russian officer, whom Marquez had met somewhere in Europe, and who had been in the Spanish service and in the war in Morocco. He was an agreeable and intelligent man, but of his military talents very little can be said. The Mexican officers on the staff of Marquez are not even worth mentioning.

With General Marquez was also Colonel Don Miguel Lopez, who went to Querétaro to resume the command of his regiment of the Empress, which had been transferred to that city.

Lopez, who by his black treason has given his infamous name to the pillory for all time, is a tall, portly man, of some thirty years of age, who does not look like a Mexican. His round head is covered with fair hair, rather thin in the middle, and arranged so as to cover deficiencies by the aid of long side hair; his moustaches and short royal are also fair. He looked very well in his red hussar jacket, trimmed with black, and the more so, as his manners were gentlemanly and elegant. Besides wearing several Mexican orders, he was decorated with the officer's cross of the Legion of Honour. He was always extremely well mounted with

American horses, and his whole appearance made a favourable impression.

The Emperor was also accompanied by a member of his cabinet, Don Garcia Aguirre, Secretary of the Interior. He is an aristocratic looking, excellent, honest gentleman, and was a staunch and faithful servant of the Emperor. He was very religious, and when later in prison with me he always officiated at mass.

The aides of the Emperor were Colonel Don Pedro Ormachea, a nephew of the Bishop Ormachea of Tulancingo, and Lieut.-Colonel Don Augustin Pradillo. The military chaplain of the headquarters was Luis G. Aguere; physician of the Emperor, Dr. S. Basch; and private secretary, Mr. Luis Blasio. Besides these gentlemen the Emperor had with him an Hungarian cook and four Mexican servants.

It had been stated, that the troops accompanying the Emperor would amount to ten thousand men; and I was very much disappointed on observing that he had only one thousand six hundred men, and eighteen smooth-bored guns!

This little army was composed of detachments of eleven different corps. The best troops amongst them were the municipal guards of the city and the valley of Mexico, on foot and on horseback; the Espladores of the valley of Mexico, and the small detachment of the regiment Khevenhüller. All the municipal guards were commanded by Colonel Don Antonio Diaz, and those on foot under Lieut.-Colonel Don Juaquin Rodriguez, the bravest soldier I ever saw. The Espladores were commanded by a Spaniard, Captain Don Antonio Gonzales. These and the municipal guards formed, during the whole march to Querétaro, our advanced guard, and with them were always the Emperor and General Marquez. Half the troops were raw Mexican recruits, more inclined to earn their pay by running away than by fighting.

On the 14th of February we marched to Tepeji del Rio, and on the 15th to San Francisco Zoyaniquilpam, and from thence, on the 16th, to Arroyo Zarco. At seven o'clock in the morning, half a league from the village of San Miguel Calpulalpam, we came upon the outposts of the enemy, who soon retired to a defile on the other side of the village; a very strong position, which could not have been forced by us, if it had been defended by a better enemy.

Our troops now halted, under the usual precautions, in the village for breakfast, and after an hour's repose the Emperor placed himself at our head, and led us to the attack.

After some lively skirmishing the municipal guard, on foot, under the brave Rodriguez, advanced to take the heights to the right of the gorge, whilst our artillery fired with shells against a conical hill on its left, which we could not attack otherwise for want of troops. Though this artillery fire checked the enemy somewhat, it did not prevent him from firing into our attacking forces, inflicting some losses on them.

Rodriguez, however, carried the heights and the defile after a sharp fight of about an hour's duration.

The Emperor was always in the middle of the fight, and distinguished himself by his coolness. I was close to his Majesty when I heard some one blubbering. I looked round, and saw that it came from the poor Hungarian cook. A spent ball from the height passed through his upper lip, and knocked out some of his teeth. They must have been strong teeth, for the bullet remained in the mouth, and the cook, who did not like the taste of lead, spit it out together with his ivories. By this his tasting faculties were spoiled for some time.

When we had passed the conquered defile, we were attacked on our left flank by guerillas, who appeared on the plains. The detachment of the Espladores and another of the ninth cavalry, under Major Malburg, advanced to drive them off, and I joined the attack. One of the enemy whom I pursued jumped over a stone wall, and tumbled down with his horse on the other side. I cleared the fence immediately after him to take him prisoner, but he got up and aimed his carbine at me, at three paces' distance. I had just time to fire, and sent a bullet through his head, which entered over his right eye. Though he fell dead on his face, the soldiers that followed me ran their lances and bullets through his body, according to the bad Mexican fashion.

The enemy now retired, and did not molest us again on our march to Querétaro. We had captured a number of prisoners, whom General Marquez would have shot immediately, but the Emperor forbade this. Report, however, said that Marquez despatched them secretly during the night, and it would have been just like him.

Next morning, at six o'clock, we marched from Arroyo Zarco to San Juan del Rio, and from thence to Colorado, which is only four leagues from Querétaro.

During the march the Emperor ordered me frequently to his side, and conversed with me for hours. He spoke about the general position of affairs, his hopes and expectations, and made some confidential communications to me.

During these hours passed at the side of the Emperor I had a good opportunity of observing Marquez, who generally rode alone by himself, absorbed in thought, which could not have been of a very pleasant or innocent character, as his face wore a rather sinister expression.

When the Emperor wanted to speak to him, Marquez generally heard only at the second or third call, and was then like one awakened from a dream. His face changed at once to a disagreeable, exaggerated friendliness, and he approached the Emperor like a fawning dog.

OCCUPATION OF QUERETARO.

WE arrived before Querétaro on the 19th of February, at ten o'clock a.m. This city had been always very friendly to the cause of the Emperor, and the news of his arrival produced amongst its inhabitants a very agreeable excitement. Young and old, men and women, came out to meet him on the Cuesta China, a rather high hill south of the city, and about 800 metres from the toll-house of the Garita de Mejico. The Emperor and his little army were greeted with a heartfelt enthusiasm by the people.

The garrison was marched up between the Cuesta China and the garita, and at their head were the Generals Miramon, Escobar, the Prefeet of the City, Mejia, Castillo, Arellano, Valdez, Casanova, and a great number of other officers. Miramon and Escobar greeted the Emperor with an appropriate speech, and he replied in the same manner.

This over, the Emperor entered the city, which was decked out with flags and otherwise, and rode to the Casino, where he took up his quarters. On entering that place his horse stumbled, which has been considered since olden times as a bad omen, but nobody noticed it much in the joyful excitement of that hour.

The Emperor soon after received the higher clergy and the authorities of the city, and a number of officers were presented to him. He then proceeded on foot to the cathedral, where a solemn *Te Deum* was celebrated.

Before continuing my narrative, I think it may be well to say a few words about the personages who met the Emperor here, and who were to play an important part in the following tragedy.

Don Miguel Miramon was the most important amongst them. As I have said before, he had been one of the most prominent chiefs of the Church party, and even President of the Republic in his twenty-fifth year. He was now a handsome man of about thirty-four or five, of middling height, elegant in figure and manner, and with dark hair, moustaches, and royal. He was a man of great intellect, extremely ambitious, very brave and daring, but no scientific general, and rather an indifferent strategist.

From Orizaba, where he with Marquez and Father Fischer, induced the Emperor to stay, he went in the middle of December, 1866, to Mexico, collected in haste from four to five hundred men, and with these and a battery he marched towards the northern State of Zacatecas, to prevent the enemy from concentrating their troops, and to advance with them over Querétaro to Mexico, as they intended. General Don Severo del Castillo had received orders from him to move in the same direction, and to co-operate with him; and General Don Thomas Mejia, who had been compelled to give up San Luis Potosi, was also on his march towards Querétaro.

The capital of the State of Zacatecas, of the same name, was then the seat of the Republican Government, and Juarez himself was in the city. This opportunity was too tempting for the bold young general, who had increased his forces by some troops which he had taken with him when passing Querétaro, and by recruiting on his march; and he resolved on a *coup de main* without waiting for the forces of Castillo, who were still at some distance.

The bold plan succeeded admirably. The enemy in Zacatecas was most completely surprised, and utterly routed. A great many prisoners, twenty guns, and a number of important papers and documents, belonging to the Republican Government, were the fruit of this brilliant victory. Juarez was nearly taken prisoner, and escaped in a carriage. It must have been expected that they would capture him, as the Emperor had sent Miramon a strict written order, .to treat Juarez, if he should take him prisoner, in the most friendly manner, and to send him to Mexico.

The Imperial gendarmes, who were for the most part Frenchmen, committed some excesses, which were severely censured by Miramon whenever he heard of them. Amongst other things —one which infuriated the Liberals very much —they tied a rope round the neck of a bust of Juarez, and dragged it through the streets of Zacatecas.

Before Castillo had come up, the city was again attacked by a much superior Liberal force, and Miramon was compelled to evacuate it in haste.

Two days after this evacuation, when on his retreat towards Querétaro, and near the hacienda San Jacinto, the troops of Miramon were attacked in the rear and on both flanks by superior forces under Escobedo. The àttack was so sudden, that he lost his whole artillery and army, and was glad to escape with a few officers, who had good and fast horses, to Querétaro, where he joined Mejia and Castillo.

His younger brother, General Don Joaquin Miramon, was not so fortunate. He was severely wounded, and taken prisoner. Escobedo dragged him on his march from one place to another, until a few leagues from San Luis Potosi. Here, in the evening, the order was given to shoot him. As the unhappy man was unable to walk, he was carried in an arm-chair to the place of execution, and as it was already dark, shot *a bout portant*. To see whether he was really dead, some matches were lighted, which were blown out several times by the wind. The general moved still, and some officers who were present amused themselves with firing their revolvers into his body. His head was scattered, and his body pierced by thirty bullets.

At San Jacinto, one hundred and twenty-three Frenchmen were taken also, and amongst them those gendarmes who had insulted the bust of Juarez. They had been kept for several days in a place where they had much liberty, and the light-hearted Frenchmen had no foreboding of the awful doom which awaited them. One day spirits were distributed amongst them, and they were told that they were to be taken to some other place, but, as they had to pass through the Liberal army, their eyes were to be bandaged. As this is frequently done, they suspected nothing, and marched blindfolded for half an hour, when they were permitted to take away the bands. They here found themselves in an interior yard of the hacienda San Jacinto, opposite two battalions of infantry, and were informed that they were to die by the order of the Supreme Government. It was an awful, heartrending scene. Ten prisoners were always shot together, the rest looking on. The bodies, frequently still quivering, were thrown into a waggon, and with the blood dripping from it, drove past the poor condemned out of the hacienda, to return immediately for a fresh load.

This horrible butchery lasted longer than an hour, as it was interrupted by an incident which illustrated, still more than even this bloody execution, the unfeeling cruelty of the Mexicans. The soldiers did not aim well, and it happened that one of a lot of ten—Hippolite Rolin was his name—was left unharmed by the first volley. He jumped away, but was captured, and added to the next lot. This time he was only slightly wounded, and escaped. He was caught again, his feet were tied, and he was shot at the shortest distance!

All these details I have from a Liberal officer, who was present at this scene, which has scarcely its equal in the first French Revolutien.

Don Thomas Mejia was a little ugly Indian, remarkably yellow, of about forty-five, with an enormous mouth, and over it a few black bristles, representing a moustache. He was a thoroughly honest, reliable man, devoted to the Emperor, a very good general of cavalry, and well known for his personal bravery. Before an attack, it was his habit to take a lance from one of his soldiers, and rush with it, amongst the first, on the line of the enemy. Some years ago he took Querétaro from the Liberals. On his entering the city, its last defenders fled to the first story of the town hall. Mejia appeared in front of it, at the head of his cavalry. Lance in hand, he rode up the steps, and in the large hall made the Liberals prisoners, and then rode to the balcony, welcoming with an hurrah his victorious troops.

Don Severo Castillo is a little, black-haired, very thin and delicate man, and almost deaf. In former years he had the misfortune of falling into the hands of the Liberals, and the rough treatment he had to undergo destroyed his health for ever. They sent him [as a prisoner to the Isla de Caballos, a rocky island in the Pacific, which is so unhealthy that nobody can live there more than a year or two. The place is so barren, that it does not produce any kind of food, and fresh meat and flour was brought to the prisoners by fishermen at certain times. Castillo passed a whole year alone on this island.

He had made himself a hut of cactus, and slept on seaweed. At last he escaped from this horrid place by the help of a fisherman.

Castillo was an honest, brave, and reliable friend of the Emperor. He is a thoroughly educated soldier, and his coolness in the midst of battle is quite admirable. Fear is such a stranger to him, that he even under fire gives his orders as coolly and composedly as if he were in his room at home. In my opinion he is the best strategist of all the Mexican generals.

Don Ramirez Arellano was a very agreeable, well-educated gentleman, of about thirty years of age, with a very dark complexion, and a smart black moustache. He is a very good artillery officer, and became later chief of all the artillery in Querétaro.

On the march already in San Juan del Rio, the Emperor issued an army order, which was read to all the troops in Querétaro. In this order he informed the army that he placed himself at its head; that he longed for this day, in order to fight for the two most holy causes—independence and restoration of order. Free from "foreign pressure" and influence, they might do their best for the honour of the national flag.

On the 21st February, the commanders of

Joh. Lindner München sc.

the different corps were invited to dinner with
the Emperor. I received, also, an invitation,
and had my place at the side of Lopez, who
carried on a very lively conversation with his
Majesty, who sat opposite us. Lopez made
himself very agreeable that day, and no one
who listened to him, and observed him, would
ever have thought that this man would become
the Judas of Querétaro.

On the 22nd, the Emperor, accompanied by
his generals, rode to the garita of Celaya, to
receive General Mendez, who was to arrive from
Michuacan with four thousand men.

Don Ramon Mendez was a little, plump
Indian, with a rather handsome face and dark
brown hair and beard, who looked very well in
his red Mexican hussar jacket. He wore a
sombrero like the Emperor, and was decorated,
besides the Mexican orders, with the officer's
cross of the French Legion of Honour, which,
besides him in the army, only Mejia, Lopez,
and a General Calvo had. Mendez was a
very good partisan, very brave, and idolized
by his soldiers, but, unfortunately, inclined to
cruelty. He was devoted to the Emperor, but
a decided enemy of Miramon, whom he distrusted, and of whom he said, that he cared little
either for empire or Emperor, but only for himself and his ambitious plans: an opinion pretty

generally entertained, which, however, in the case of Mendez, might have been strengthened by some jealousy.

On the afternoon of the same day, a review, commanded by Miramon, of all the troops in Querétaro, was held, except those of Mendez, who were tired from their march. These troops consisted of one thousand six hundred men, under Marquez; those which came with Miramon and Castillo from Zacatecas—viz., the battalions of the Cazadores del Emperador and Tiradores, the 7th battalion of the line, the balance of the 5th, the gendarmes, the 8th regiment of cavalry, the regiment of the Empress (horse), and two field and one mountain battery — about five thousand men. Thus, our whole force consisted of nine thousand men and thirty-nine guns.

After this review, the Emperor distributed some decorations amongst those soldiers who had distinguished themselves in a fight at the Quemada, in which brave Mejia had beaten the Liberals on his march from St. Luis Potosi.

On the 23rd of February, a solemn mass and requiem was held, in memory of the cruelly-murdered General Miramon, which was attended by the Emperor, and the army received orders to wear mourning for eight days.

On the 24th the Emperor divided the army in the following manner : The whole of the infantry was commanded by Miramon. This consisted of two divisions under Mendez and Castillo. The whole cavalry was commanded by Mejia, and the artillery by Arellano. Marquez became chief of the general staff, and General Vidaurri was made deputy of the Secretary of Finance, and commenced by making in Querétaro a forced loan of sixty thousand piastres, as money was now a positive necessity. The ministers in Mexico had promised heaps of gold, and laid before the Emperor doubtful financial statements. Instead of the millions which they had promised in Orizaba, and later, they procured with the utmost trouble the before-mentioned fifty thousand pesos for the campaign of Querétaro, and sent from Mexico only once nineteen thousand pesos, which lasted a few days only.

On this day a council of war was also held, in which it was resolved to send strict orders to General Tabera, who was left in command of the capital, to send all foreign troops then in Mexico, together with the required ammunition and ambulances and one hundred thousand pesos to Querétaro. On the march already similar orders had been given, but had been disregarded by the ministers.

The troops to be sent from Mexico were: the hussar regiment of Count Khevenhüller (all Austrians), the battalion of Baron von Ham-

merstein (also Austrians), from four to five
hundred men strong; the gendarmes of the
guard, under Count Wickenburg; the Cazadores
a caballo—all foreigners under Majors Gerloni
and Czismadai, and also eight rifled guns.

On the afternoon of February 25th, the
troops of Mendez were passed in review. They
were the best Mexican troops in the army of the
Emperor, whom they had served already for
several years, fighting independent from the
French in the State of Michuacan. They consisted of the 1st, 2nd, 3rd, and 4th battalions
of the line, the 4th and 5th regiments of cavalry,
one field and one mountain battery.

Before resuming, it is necessary to say a
few words about the city of Querétaro and its
different localities.

Querétaro is the capital of the State named
after it, and is situated on the southern side of
the little river of Rio Blanca, which flows from
the east to the west, and, below the city, makes
a turn towards the south. The city has between
forty and fifty thousand inhabitants, and forms
not quite a regular quadrangle of two thousand
four hundred metres in length, and one thousand
two hundred metres in width. It is built in a
valley of which the opposite heights may be
mutually reached by cannon shot.

On the north side of the little river is the

suburb San Luis, with its gardens ascending up a hill, about one hundred and fifty metres high, called Cerro San Gregorio. Another much higher hill, Cerro San Pablo, runs north from San Gregorio, in a parallel direction, and is divided from it by a valley of one thousand to one thousand two hundred metres wide.

Behind San Pablo rises Cerro la Cantara, which runs towards the east, and with a sweep in a southern direction, approaches the Rio Blanca within fifty or one hundred metres above the city.

Opposite this end of La Cantara, on the southern bank of Rio Blanca, and quite close to it, rises a hilly range which runs in a southwestern direction, and forms a curve reaching to the western end of the city, from which it is separated by a plain of eight hundred to one thousand metres wide. This range is called Cerro el Cimatario, with different names for its different parts. One of these parts, and the highest, is the Cuesta China, over which runs the road from Mexico.

At the western end of El Cimatario, nearer to the city, is another isolated hill called El Jacal. West of the city extends a plain, in the middle of which is a small, isolated rocky hill overgrown with cactus, called Cerro de la Campaña (Bell hill), about one thousand five hundred metres distant from the city.

From this description it will be seen, that Querétaro is the worst place in the world to defend, as every house may be reached by gunshot from the surrounding hills. Such a defence could only be made by an army numerous enough to occupy these hills.

The highest point of the city itself is in its south-eastern corner, where on a not very high rock is built the rather extensive Colegio de la Santa Cruz, commonly called the Cruz. In the south-western corner is the Garita (gate) del Pueblito, and close to it the Casa Blanca. Between it and the cruz is the Alameda, a not very large public square for promenading, to be found in every town or city of Spanish origin.

The river which separates the city from the above-mentioned suburb San Luis, is fordable at different places, and has only one bridge at the end of the Calle Miraflores, one of the principal streets of Querétaro, which passes right through the centre of the city, and com-, menees at the north-west corner of the Alameda. The city has a great many churches, chapels, and convents, and offers a very picturesque view.

Until the 1st of March, the time was passed in many preparations, and waiting for news from Mexico. We saw nothing of the enemy, and heard but little.

The new Secretary of Finance tried to bring

about regularly the payment of the soldiers, and also as to the commissary department. This he did so successfully that the soldiers were not only satisfied, but delighted, for such a regular state of things was quite miraculous in a Mexican army.

As I am rather an indifferent financier, I could not assist General Vidaurri in his very onerous though beneficent task; and having no duty whatever, I passed my time as well as I could until the booming of the guns again set my faculties at play.

I visited the theatre Iturbide in the Calle Miraflores, where some Spanish comedies were represented rather indifferently, and where later the saddest tragedy of the century was to be enacted.

During these days a bull fight took place in an arena near the Alameda. The arena was crowded to its utmost, and I was also there. The Emperor, however, who was formerly enthusiastic about this sport when travelling in Spain, did not go to see the bull fight, probably not expecting much. It was, indeed, a paltry affair, though bloody enough. Six horses were gored, but neither the picadores nor matadores showed any skill.

I must, however, not forget a half-disgusting half-laughable incident, which took place at this

fight.   Two women appeared in the arena to try
their skill against a bull whose horns were provided with balls.   The rough-looking, though
rather pretty women did not earn much glory,
however; much bruised and with torn garments
they were compelled to fly from the arena, followed by the derisive laughter and hissing of
the audience.

On the 1st of March the Emperor held a
review of Mejia's cavalry, which, for a Mexican
troop, was very excellent.   The horses looked
extremely well fed and clean, and the uniforms
of the soldiers were better than usual.   The
best troops amongst them were the regiment
Quiroga—mostly consisting of Vidaurri men, who
formerly fought against Mejia, until they came
over with their old chieftain to the party of the
Emperor; then the regiment of the Empress,
and the 5th regiment.

Cavalry patrols had scoured the country
around to get news from the enemy; and from
farmers, and especially from priests they heard,
though only as a report, that masses of Liberals
were concentrating in St. Martin, between Querétaro and San Luis Potosi; and others at Celaya,
about four or five leagues from Querétaro.

On the afternoon of the 2nd of March, I had
to make a report to the Emperor.   As he was
just going out for a promenade on horseback he

invited me to accompany him to the Alameda. When on our way an officer handed him a despatch from Mexico, which had just arrived.

After he had read it, he said, " Now look at these blackguards! (meaning his ministers in Mexico,) these fellows are afraid, and will not send me any troops. They say the capital was in danger. They are only afraid for themselves!"

The news of the advance of the enemy was confirmed in the afternoon of the 4th of March, and on the 5th, towards night, they were seen concentrating in the plain west of the Cerro de la Campaña, and our outposts were reinforced. During the night of the 5th to the 6th of March the garrison was alarmed, as an attack was expected at dawn. Our position, which we kept for some time, was as following :

The centre and key point was the Cerro de la Campaña, which falls off rather steeply towards the west. Here the Emperor and Miramon took up their position, with one battalion and two batteries. Between this cerro and that of St. Gregorio, on which was placed a battery, stood the division Castillo. To the left of the Cerro de la Campaña, between it and the Casa Blanca, near the Garita de Pueblito, were posted the division Mendez, protecting thus the road coming from Celaya. Between the Casa Blanca and the Alameda stood, in columns, our cavalry, under. Mejia; its left flank protected by two regiments.

In the morning the enemy was seen moving in the plain west of the Campaña, but no attack was intended; they merely occupied the villages and haciendas in the neighbourhood.

From that time the Emperor remained on the Cerro de la Campaña, and slept this and the following nights on the ground, covered only with his plaid, and over him the starry sky; Miramon and Marquez, who were with him, did the same. The hill was cleared from the cactus plants, with which it was overgrown, some breastworks, and six or seven embankments for guns were built.

The cavalry skirmishers surrounding the army of the enemy, who then consisted of eighteen thousand men, commanded by General Escobedo, approached our lines to within five hundred to six hundred paces. General Vidaurri, who was both Secretary of Finance and of War in the field, had his hands quite fully occupied in providing for the troops, and with making financial arrangements, in which I could not assist him; I, therefore, kept always near the Emperor without having any particular duty.

On the morning of the 7th March an attack was expected with the more certainty, as the enemy was seen massing his troops in the plain. We became, however, soon aware that it was only for a review.

Several generals advised the Emperor to attack the Liberals in this position with all available forces, and he was much inclined to do so; but Marquez opposed this enterprise, and said that the enemy would not wait for our attack in the plain, and that it would also be better to let him collect all his forces, to annihilate them with one stroke!

The wisdom of this silly advice was explained to me at length by Marquez's Russian military assistant, who considered my reasons for an immediate attack as pedantry.

The following days passed away by our waiting impatiently for an attack, and with movements of the army of the enemy, in which he was not hindered by us.

Our ·chief of staff, Marquez, must have imagined that the little Rio Blanca was a sufficient protection for our right flank, for he neglected to occupy the Cerro San Pablo, which commanded the city. This negligence was soon noticed by the enemy, who occupied the garita on the road towards the north, situated at the foot of the Pablo, and also the chapel on the top of this hill, on the night between the 8th and 9th of March. As this position might become

very troublesome for our right flank, General
Mendez made a reconnaissance in force in this
direction, with the regiment of the Empress and
the hussars. After a little skirmish in the
valley between San Gregorio and San Pablo, he
retired. In consequence of this reconnaissance,
General Castillo advanced next morning, with
one brigade, against San Pablo, his flank
covered by cavalry. The battalion of the
Cazadores, who were at the head, chased the
infantry of the enemy from the garita, stormed
the hill San Pablo, with its chapel, and retired,
after having discovered on the other side of the
hill several thousand infantry. In this attack
the commander of the Cazadores, Lieut.-
Colonel Villasana, was wounded.

The Emperor sent for me at noon. As I
had commanded a brigade in the United States'
army, he excused himself for asking me whether
I would accept the command of the Cazadores,
as no brigade was vacant. The corps, whose
command he offered me, he said, was a select
one, and could be managed only by great energy.
As I was utterly tired of my position without
any definite duty, I accepted it with pleasure.
My commission was drawn out immediately, and
the major in charge presented me to the battalion.

I was well received by both officers and
soldiers, though the major was perhaps a little

dissatisfied, as he might have expected to be promoted himself. The Cazadores consisted of nearly seven hundred men, of whom the greater part were French ; but there were also Germans, Hungarians, and about a hundred and fifty Mexicans. It was a wild corps of the bravest soldiers that could be found. The battalion stood in the centre of the position of General Castillo, near the road from Querétaro to San Luis Potosi, and four twelve-pounders were attached to it.

In the afternoon lively movements were seen amongst the enemy. The heights of San Pablo and La Cantara were occupied by them, and the same was the case with that of the Cuesta China, where they constructed a battery. Nothing was done to impede these movements, but it was thought advisable to change our position. General Castillo fell back behind the Rio Blanca, and occupied the whole line of the river along the city. A brigade of General Mendez's division was sent to the Convent de la Cruz, where the Emperor took up his head-quarters, and where he was followed by his chief of staff, Marquez. The cavalry under Mejia remained in their former position.

In consequence of these changes, I and my Cazadores were charged with the defence of the bridge at the end of the Calle Miraflores.

On the same evening, about six o'clock, the enemy opened fire against the cruz from his battery on the Cuesta China.

As the cruz will occupy from this time the most prominent part in the siege of Querétaro, a description of it will be required.

The extensive convent, Santa Cruz, which stands on the rock on the south-eastern corner of the city, and commands it, dates from the time of the Conquest, and is built of very solid stone, against which cannon-shot makes but little impression.

The length of the whole building is little more than six hundred metres, and its width about four hundred. The whole is surrounded with a solid stone wall. Another wall divides the whole area into two parts. The western division, which is only two hundred and sixty metres long, contains on its northern half the convent, the southern half is occupied by different yards. The eastern half of the area belonging to the convent is occupied by a large yard, which would be rectangular also, if its northern wall did not form a projecting angle. On the eastern wall, projecting outside, stands a solid stone building, called the pantheon. It is the burial place of the convent, and at its southern side is a chapel. As the ground slopes down from the east towards the west, this pantheon, with its chapel, stands on the highest point of the city. On the west side, before the convent, is a square, called Plaza de la Cruz.

From this description it will be seen that the cruz may be considered as the citadel of Querétaro.

When General Marquez arranged for the defence of the cruz, he left the pantheon and its chapel unoccupied, and when the Emperor and other persons remonstrated, he said, " that they did not know the enemy with whom they had to deal." Marquez had always told the Emperor that the army of the Liberals was nothing but a worthless rabble.

THE 14th of March is, in the siege of Querétaro, a very memorable and glorious day.
Movements in the army of the enemy in the
morning indicated that a general attack was
intended, and this really took place, at about
ten o'clock a.m., against three different points:
the cruz, the bridge, and the position between
the Alameda, and the Casa Blanca, which latter
was occupied by the cavalry, under Mejia. A
fourth attack against the Cerro de la Campaña
was only a feint.

As soon as the batteries of the Cuesta China
had given the signal, strong columns of cavalry
advanced from the south against the Casa Blanca
and Alameda. When they arrived on the plain
before them, Mejia attacked them with his
cavalry, and with such impetuosity, that the
enemy, after a short resistance, fled in great
disorder. Our cavalry pursued them beyond
the Cerro Cimatario, which offers no impediments to the movements of cavalry, and drove
them to their camp, near the Estancia de las

Vacas, killing and wounding one hundred and thirty men, and making seventy prisoners.

Supported by a tremendous fire from the Cuesta China, dense columns of infantry now advanced against the eastern side of the cruz, and, thanks to the stupid or treacherous negligence of Marquez, the unoccupied pantheon chapel was stormed, its walls towards the yard provided with loopholes, and the azotea or flat roof of the chapel occupied with soldiers, who fired from their elevated position against our troops who defended the convent.

Before relating the attack against the bridge, I must describe the ground. Along the river runs a street. The flat roofs of the houses next the bridge had been provided by General Castillo with breastworks during the previous night. This side the bridge, leaving only a narrow passage for one man abreast, was raised a battery of adobes, which are bricks made of sun-dried clay, of a foot square and four inches thick. Between two walls made by them earth was filled in, and this wall contained embrasures for three twelve-pounders, one of which raked the bridge. On the other side of the bridge, in the suburb San Luis, ran also a street along the river, and there was a free space directly before the bridge of about one hundred paces' length. At the south-west corner of this open place, therefore, next the bridge, stood an extensive building, called meson, an inn for muleteers and such people, with a corral surrounded by a solid stone wall. Before the houses opposite the bridge, on the north side of the free place, stands a well, and to the right and left of them two not quite parallel streets run up the slope of the Cerro San Gregorio, on which the suburb is built. The next street, running parallel to the river, and intersecting the two above mentioned, leads to the right to the church of San Sebastian, and from it runs another street down to the river. The church stands on higher ground, and from the gallery of its steeple one can see directly into the streets of Querétaro, and sharpshooters may reach them with their guns.

At the signal given from the Cuesta China, columns of infantry moved down the two streets, formed on the square, and advanced against the bridge. At a distance of one hundred paces they were received with a shower of canister and bullets, which made them turn tail at once, and retire behind the church of San Sebastian. Cautioned by the warm reception at the bridge, they moved down the street leading from the church to the river, and where it is fordable. As soon as their intention was noticed by General Castillo, I received orders to meet them with my Cazadores, whilst the bridge remained occupied by our reserve, the battalion Celaya.

In double quick time I marched through the next street behind me, and was just in time to pour one volley after the other into them, whilst the right wing gun of the bridge battery greeted them with canister shots. They had to retire for a second time.

Though the enemy must have suffered considerable losses, they again attacked the bridge with renewed force between eleven and twelve o'clock, and succeeded in occupying some of the opposite houses, and also the Meson Sebastian, from which they kept up a rather lively fire, to which we responded.

Whilst this useless firing was going on at the bridge, the fight was continued at the cruz. Supported by the guns of the Cuesta China, which sent over the cruz and its yards a shower of shot and shell, the infantry in the pantheon, and from the roof of the chapel, fired against the convent and about forty men who had placed themselves in a very exposed position on its roof. They were commanded by an Austrian captain of the name of Linger, whom General Thun used to call the captain with the Bordeaux nose and the Mayonnaise face. Notwithstanding his remarkable complexion, he was a very brave man, and kept his dangerous place with great courage, until he was killed by a bullet entering his forehead, after which his men left the position. No longer hindered by them, the enemy tried to advance into the large yard, protected by densely-growing cactus plants, with which the ground was covered. This protection, though sufficient against the eyes, was not sufficient against the bullets from the convent, and the ·enemy had to fall back again to the pantheon.

About the same time the cavalry of the enemy, opposite the Alameda and Casa Blanca, had recovered from the beating they received from Mejia, and made a second attack, but fared still worse than the first time. Brave Mejia, always the foremost, made a very brilliant charge, and drove them back between Cerro Cimatario and El Jacal. Here they lost several hundreds of dead, wounded, and prisouers.

Had Mejia availed himself of his glorious success to attack the battery of the Cuesta China in the flank, which attack would have been supported by the guns from the cruz, the victory of this day would have been still more complete. But I believe brave Mejia felt a little astonished at the unusual pluck of the enemy: at least, I heard him say to the Emperor, that as long as he had been fighting in Mexico he had never seen the Liberals in such force and perfection.

During the fight on the cruz the Emperor was on the Plaza de la Cruz, exposed to shot and shell sent in abundance from the Cuesta China. All remonstrances proved as useless as those made by a deputation of the generals the day before, who besought him not to expose himself so much. Bold Mejia said, in his plain language, " Consider, your Majesty, if you are killed all of us will fight against each other for the presidency ;" but, though these words made some impression on the Emperor, he said that the place where he stood was the right place for him.

The lull in the fight at the bridge, interrupted only by firing from the houses, was of no long duration. A little after noon great masses of infantry were seen forming near the Chapel de la Cruz del Cerro, which is higher up the slope of San Gregorio, at the end of the suburb, and at the same time a rifled Parrot gun, placed in the street to the left of the place before the bridge, commenced firing with shells against the battery at the bridge, raking at the same time the Calle Miraflores, and reaching even the Plaza de Armos, in the centre of the city, where several citizens were killed.

When the shells burst amongst us, my Caza-

dores, elated by their success, became impatient.
They surrounded me, crying, " Lead on, colonel;
lead on! we will whip them. The Cazadores
always go a-head!"

In Europe it would be difficult to imagine
such a corps. The wild fellows were always
fighting among themselves, and I had to do all
in my power to prevent bloodshed and murder;
but as soon as they were led against the enemy,
they were like one man, and every one tried to
outdo his comrades in daring deeds. Even the
very buglers, boys between fourteen and sixteen, stole sometimes outside the lines, armed
with a gun and a box full of cartridges, to hunt
" Chinacos " (Liberals) on their own hook.

I comforted my Cazadores as well as I
could by promising them that the right moment
was near at hand; and I soon received the
most welcome order from my brigadier, General
Valdez, to drive away the troublesome Parrot
gun, and to occupy the meson and adjacent
houses, whilst the battalion Celaya was to
occupy our position. The cavalry regiment
Empress, commanded by Colonel Lopez, received orders to protect our left flank.

I thought it well to address my impatient
boys, and made a speech to them still more
effective than any of those with which I once
encouraged my soldiers in the United States,

then in broken English, now I did it in still more broken Spanish. I told them that I did not want to hear a shot until I ordered it, and that the main business had to be done with the bayonet alone. I then formed them for the attack, keeping them under cover as long as possible. While I did so, my men actually quivered with eagerness, like a pack of hounds waiting for the signal. With a tremendous cheer, in as many languages as were spoken around the tower of Babel, and a "*Viva il Emperador,*" they stormed the bridge and road before it. When we had reached about the middle of the place, we received a shower of canister at a distance of fifty paces, and discovered the dangerous Parrot before us. I raised my sword, and calling out, "*Viva il Emperador! a la pieza muchachos!*" we rushed up to the gun. My major, Don Macedonio Victorica, and a little swarthy Mexican, were close at my heels. The brave Liberal commander of the gun, a lieutenant, fired at the major with his revolver, and wounded him severely; but it was his last shot, half a dozen bayonets were immediately buried in his body. All the artillerymen belonging to the rifled cannon were bayoneted or killed with the stock of the guns used like clubs. The conquered piece was sent back to the bridge, whilst the

battalion Celaya fired on the Liberals in the
meson, who soon saved themselves, and fled
through the gardens up the hill. The infantry
we saw before us fled panic-struck into the
houses, of which they locked the doors; but I
advanced into the street to dislodge them, and
the doors were opened by well-applied shots.

There were many wild deeds done in those
houses which I could not hinder, though I tried
to do so. The French in the Cazadores, infuriated by the butchery of San Jacinto, had
promised themselves to spare no enemy, and
least of all Frenchmen who served with the
Liberals. They made good their word in the
most horrid manner, and I had even to use my
sword against some of my men, who would not
obey my orders to spare those that cried for
mercy. At some of the thresholds the dead
were piled up, and in one of the houses was per-
formed a most singular and cruel scene. One
of my sergeants, a Frenchman, had killed in a
house four Mexicans; a fifth man, a Frenchman,
was on his knees praying for mercy. His con-
queror, in charging his musket, said, " All the
mercy I will grant you is, that I will not despatch you like a dog, but give you the honour
of a bullet." With that he very calmly shot
his countryman dead.

The stampede which I saw amongst the

dense mass of the enemy before me, induced me to follow up my success. Driving them before me like a flock of sheep, I turned the next corner in the street leading to San Sebastian, and then, following again the street leading up hill, we arrived at the chapel De la Cruz del Cerro, at the end of the suburb San Luis. From this position I saw that the enemy had formed again at the chapel San Trinidad, which was to my right, a little higher up San Gregorio. Before they succeeded, however, I had drawn up my battalion in line of battle, placing a company in reserve, and I poured volley after volley into the enemy, who fled over the edge of the hill in great disorder. At this moment I saw emerging from a street the head of the regiment Empress, under Lopez. I sent him two officers with the request that he would pursue the enemy, and when he refused I rode up to him myself and repeated my request, but he answered, " That he could not expose his regiment in such a manner, and that the ground was not fit for cavalry." If he could not use his cavalry on that ground, I cannot see of what use he was there. I have myself been an officer of cavalry in Prussia, and know very well where cavalry may be used. The ground was certainly not so smooth as a parade-ground, but it was practicable.

As I had only orders to silence the Parrot gun, and to take the meson, which was satisfactorily accomplished, I dared not to transgress further without waiting for orders. I therefore sent Lieutenant Montecon, my aide, to General Valdez, to report our success and position, and to request him to send another battalion, that I might take and maintain San Gregorio.

General Valdez, however, sent me, with his congratulations, the order to retreat, as a further advance was against his instructions, and to put a company into the meson. I had of course only to obey orders, but my Cazadores were furious. They had killed more than three hundred men!

I mentioned a little black Mexican, who, with the major, was first with me at the gun. He was a very queer fellow, who showed me great attachment, and was anxious for an approving word, and happy if I gave him some dangerous commission. At every opportunity he was affected to tears, which made a very striking contrast to his wildness and bravery. During the fight he came to me crying, and holding up in his hand a thing which I recognized with difficulty as the barrel of a gun. "Colonel," he cried, "Colonel, I have done my duty—yes, I did my duty; I have deserved a new gun, or I cannot fight any more." On my questioning him as to what he had done with his gun, he said that his bayonet broke when he spitted a Chinaco against the wall, and his stock when he dashed another's brains out; but the skull of a third, whom he hit with the barrel, proved harder, and the barrel bent in the manner he showed me.

We had lost in dead and wounded about thirty men. Our retreat to the bridge was quite an ovation, and I must say I felt some satisfaction when the Cazadores cheered their new colonel. When I arrived on the place before the bridge, I met Mr. H. C. Clark, correspondent of the "New York Herald," who became so enthusiastic that he pulled me almost off my horse in giving me the Mexican embrazo. Mr. Clark was, however, no American, but a very amiable English gentleman, though correspondent of the "New York Herald," to whom I was happy enough to render some service when he came with the Emperor to Querétaro, and was ordered by Marquez, in a brutal manner, as a suspected foreigner, to leave the city. I had already known him in the United States, and he therefore applied to me in his difficulty. I spoke at once to the Emperor, who gave him a written permit to remain, whilst Mr. Clark gave me privately his word of honour not to hold any communication with the enemy, and to re-

port truthfully.   He was afterwards nearly
killed in his room by a cannon-ball.   Under renewed cheering the captured Parrot gun was
passed through our barricade and sent to the
cruz.   The Cazadores occupied their old position.   When I saw Castillo and Valdez they
congratulated me on my success, and gave me
the embrazo.

The enemy were so much scared by the
severe punishment we had inflicted on them,
that they dared not show themselves all day.
Even San Gregorio remained unoccupied; but
early next morning they had constructed a
battery there.

During our fight in San Luis, severe fighting
was also going on on the south side.   Beside
their battery on the Cuesta China, the enemy
had placed there two regiments as a reserve;
and in the plain between the city and the Cerro
Cimatario, four regiments of horse, with four
field-pieces.   As these troops were threatened
by our cavalry under Mejia, on their left flank,
another column of cavalry was sent over the
cerro to protect it.   When Mejia attacked it,
General Miramon sent from the Alameda some
infantry with four guns, which made a very successful attack, and beat even the reserves of the
enemy.

While this was being done, the Liberals in

the pantheon had received reinforcements, and advanced over the large yard to attack the convent itself. At this perilous moment the garrison of the cruz made a decisive movement. The brave Colonel Don Sefferino Rodriguez sallied out at the head of the 3rd battalion of the line, and not only drove the Liberals from the yard, but even took the pantheon and the chapel, pursuing the enemy even for some distance. The pantheon was now well garrisoned, and not lost again during the whole siege.

About five o'clock p.m., the enemy was repulsed everywhere. We lost about six hundred men, but the loss of the enemy, who had to fight in the open field, counted by thousands. We, moreover, made between seven and eight hundred prisoners, of whom a good number joined our army.

Between five and six o'clock the Emperor, followed by Miramon, Marquez, and staff, visited the lines. Wherever he came he was received with cheers, for the courage with which he exposed himself, and the friendly and appropriate words with which he acknowledged every meritorious deed, had won him the enthusiastic affection of the soldiers.

On coming to the Cazadores, he gave me his hand, and thanked the regiment in a short speech, in which he called them " the Zouaves of Mexico," on which the shouts of exultation were deafening.

For the night the battalion Celaya had taken our position, and we rested at a less exposed place; when there, a Capuchin friar came, who had the image of the Holy Virgin hanging by a rope round his neck. The Mexicans, amongst my troops, whose hands were not cleansed yet from the blood they had spilt, rushed up to the priest with exultation, crossing themselves, and devoutly kissed the image.

At last, night spread its brown mantle over the city, and the thunder of the guns and the rattling of the musketry was followed by a weird stillness. The streets were deserted, and not even a footfall was to be heard. All were sleeping after that hard day's work except the outposts. Even the clocks were silent, for it had been forgotten to wind them up; and the night watchmen, who on other nights, proclaimed the weather and the hour, snored in some corner as they did not know the time. The dogs also, which make the nights in Mexican cities only too noisy, had disappeared, allured by the horrid meal which was dished up for them outside by the grim god of war.

On the morning of the 15th we heard from deserters that the Liberals were very much discouraged by their great losses of yesterday.

The more joyous and high-spirited our men became; and when my Cazadores, who occupied again their post of honour, became aware, by the peculiar whizzing of the projectiles passing over our heads, that Santa Cruz sent its iron *cartes de visite* to San Gregorio from the mouth of the rifled gun we had taken, they exulted loudly.

All those non-commissioned officers and privates who had distinguished themselves yesterday were at noon assembled on the Plaza de la Cruz, forming a hollow square, in the middle of which stood the captured gun. To the battalion who had retaken the pantheon, and whose brave colonel had been severely wounded by a bullet in his chest, the Emperor said, " You have all behaved so bravely that I cannot make any distinction. We therefore resolved to decorate the whole battalion." This he did by attaching the cross of the Mexican eagle to their colours.

The eight Cazadores, who were first with me at the piece, received two the gold, and six the silver medal for bravery, and beside each had an ounze, that is, a new gold twenty dollar piece with the head of the Emperor on it.

The little terrible Mexican, whose water-pumps were always at work, even when he was tapping blood, had received, on my recommendation, a gold medal, and was so beside himself with pleasure that he gave me, before the whole front, the Mexican embrazo, beating with his hand my back, and shedding torrents of tears over my shoulder.

Before the assembling of the council of war, which was to have been held in the evening, I was ordered to the Emperor, who desired to hear my opinion about what was best to do under present circumstances.

I declared that I thought it best to take advantage of the discouragement produced on the enemy, by our yesterday's work, and to make an attack against San Gregorio and San Pablo with the whole of the infantry, whilst the cavalry that protected our left flank beat that of the enemy standing before the Cerro de la Campaña, and then to advance against San Luis Potosi, the temporal seat of Juarez and his government.

Hazardous, and even foolish as this proposition to attack an enemy four times more numerous, in a strong position, may appear to Europeans, it would be from want of knowledge of Mexican warfare and Mexican spirit. A defeat may, perhaps, not discourage a good European army, but with a Mexican army it is usually equal to a dissolution, even if many times larger than the conquerors. It is almost impossible to make them stand fire again. They throw away their arms, and run away to their homes, or over to the enemy.

After our success of yesterday, and the enthusiasm of our troops, I had not the slightest doubt that we should win a decisive victory, and disperse the army of the Liberals, especially if we attacked them promptly, before the arrival of the new reinforcements, which were announced.

To permit the enemy to shut us up in a place situated so unfavourably as Querétaro, which had neither a political nor strategical importance, seemed to me not only ridiculous but even fatal. Moreover, it was not in accordance with the intentions of the Emperor, and with those of Marquez either, which, at least, might be concluded from the circumstance, that Marquez left all the haciendas round Querétaro perfectly untouched, whilst the securing of their superabundance, in every kind of provision, would have been his first aim if he intended to sustain a siege. How richly these haciendas were provided was experienced by the army of the enemy, which was mostly fed by them.

If we advanced against San Luis Potosi and the west, and sent General Vidaurri to the north of the country, where his name was of the utmost importance, all the resources of those rich districts, now used by the enemy, would fall into our hands, and in a short time we should have a considerable army. Vera Cruz was still in our possession, and since the departure of the French, the revenue from the customs again became ours ; we had means for the support of such an army.

However, Marquez was of a different opinion, and his opinion was then all powerful with the Emperor. After having heard me, he said that my view of the case disagreed with that of Marquez, who had grown old in these revolutions ; who knew the country and the people ; and whose honesty and loyalty could not be doubted. Marquez had been one of the principal persons who called him to the country; and it was also Marquez who convinced him that he ought to remain in Mexico ; that he must not forsake his party, but prove that he could exist without the help of France. His honour required that he should show the world he had not degraded himself so much as to become a mere tool of another man.

The Emperor was perfectly infatuated by Marquez. Though a man of good sense, his character was too noble and too pure to suspect the honesty of others. A Napoleon and a Marquez had easy work with a nature like his. Marquez carried his point, and it was decided on being shut up in Querétaro.

·About nine o'clock p. m. (15th), the enemy had recovered so far from their panic as to attempt, under the cover of night, another attack against the bridge, but the battalion Celaya easily beat them off.

These nightly attacks against the bridge were repeated very frequently during the siege, as the bridge and the cruz were considered to be the key-points of the city. Whenever such an attack took place the city was bombarded from all their batteries, if there was not a scarcity of ammunition in the enemy's camp, as happened now and then. Liberal officers told me afterwards that they received not unfrequently ammunition by the diligence, which conveyed it to Celaya.

Ammunition, especially cannon-balls, was also not in sufficient quantity in the city, and General Arellano took care to manufacture it. We also were provided by the enemy, whose shells were very badly made, and the greater number did not explode. Men or boys who delivered a sound shell received a dollar; for a shot half a dollar was paid.

On the 16th of March the enemy must have received a fresh supply of ammunition, for they poured over the city every kind of missile. These bombardments, however, became now an every day occurrence, only enlivened now and then by some outpost skirmish. Though I saw frequently the inhabitants killed in the very streets, they became so accustomed to the bombardment that it did not generally interrupt their business. The ladies, who at the commencement kept in their houses, now made their usual afternoon promenades, and resumed their old places on the balconies, though many of them had to pay for it with their lives or limbs.

The favourite targets of the Liberal artillery were the cruz, the convent Santa Clara, occupied by our artillery-laboratory, the Cerro de la Campaña, the Alameda, Casa Blanca, and the bridge. The greatest damage was perhaps done at the cruz and the post office, which received a great many of the shot which were intended for Miramon's headquarters, which lay in the same direction, and which had been betrayed to the enemy.

Theatre and arena were closed, but all shelling could not prevent people from collecting together for their amusement. The coffee-houses were crowded, and a French one at the Plaza de Armas was the favourite resort of all officers. Here one was always sure to find the freshest news, for every one who came from a fight went there to exchange news as soon as he was free from service.

The time from 15th to 20th March was

employed in fortifying the city as well as possible, but all that could be done was to build breast-works, and to provide some buildings with embrasures and loopholes. Our batteries stood on the Cerro de la Campana; between it and the bridge, at the bridge, on the cruz, at the chapel San Francisquito, the Alameda, Casa Blanca, and between the latter and the road to Celaya. To the right of the bridge, Castillo had made some openings in a solid wall, which did not look like embrasures, but behind them he had placed mountain guns, from which the Liberals, to their great astonishment, were greeted with canister. Amongst our generals were some who were not judged able enough under present circumstances, and they were therefore removed from their commands. Amongst them were the general of division Casanova, and the brigadier-generals Herrera y Lozada and Calvo.

The Emperor sent every day for me; when he did so again on the 20th he gave me the command of the first brigade in Mendez's division, as a reward, he said, for my behaviour on the 14th. This was a very fine brigade, and consisted of the Cazadores, the 2nd, 5th, and 14th battalion of the line, the battalion of Tiradores under the command of Colonel Don Carlos Miramon, and the battalion Zamora.

On my recommendation the Emperor gave the command of the Cazadores to Major Ernest Pitner, who had been a captain in the Austrian corps. In the battle of Santa Gertrudis last year, he fell, severely wounded, into the hands of the enemy. This fight was the first success of the Liberals, and it was the more welcome to them as they captured several millions of money which were to be conveyed to Monterey. Escobedo, who won this victory and captured this money, did not forget himself. By the banking house of Brach and Schöenfeld in Monterey, he sent ten thousand pounds sterling to England for his personal account.

At the time when the Emperor marched to Querétaro, Captain Pitner was discharged, and received from Escobedo a pass to Vera Cruz, with the understanding that he should go from thence to Europe. But when the captain came to Querétaro, and saw that the Emperor had so few European officers with him, he offered his services again. Marquez treated the captain, who arrived in citizen's dress, very roughly, and had him even imprisoned as a suspicious foreigner, but when the misunderstanding was cleared up he took him as a major on his staff. Colonel Lopez received also a reserve brigade composed of different troops, and was charged especially with the defence of the cruz. Part of my brigade stood between the Cerro Campaña and the left wing of Castillo's position, and with it I had my headquarters. The other part was at the Casa Blanca with Mendez, who had left the cruz with one brigade, and now occupied the line from the Garita Pueblito to the chapel San Francisquito. I had with my brigade a battery of smooth-bored eight pounders. The gun taken on the 14th was the only rifled one in the city.

My Major del Ordenes—Don Ramon Robles —brigade-adjutant, was a stout stupid fellow, and besides him I found as an aide a Mexican lieutenant, who was still more inefficient if possible. I took therefore with me my personal aide-de-camp, Don Julian Montecon, who showed great attachment to me, and whom I loved very much. He was only seventeen, very modest and agreeable, and spoke a little French. I once said to him, that if I should be wounded or killed, he might take care of my body; and from that time he followed me in battle like my shadow, and if the fight was very sharp he was close upon my heels, as it were with open arms ready to receive me if I should be hit. The brave boy never thought of himself.

On the 20th of March an important council of war was again held, of which I have in my

possession the original record. The following
is the translation :—

*Record of the Council of War held in the Fort de
la Cruz, on the 20th of March, 1867.*

H. M. the Emperor ordered a council of
war, consisting of the undersigned generals, to
assemble at headquarters, in the Fort de la
Cruz, of the city of Querétaro, on March 20th,
1867, at three o'clock p.m. When the generals
were assembled, the sovereign said :

" Gentlemen, five different opinions about
what we have to do in our present position
have been submitted to me to-day by the
chief of artillery, our secretary of the present
council of war. We have not decided upon any
of them ; but, true to the rule laid down in Orizaba, when the Cabinet and the Council of State
resolved on our remaining at the head of the
empire, we have assembled you here, that you,
without occupying yourselves with ourselves,
but only having in view the general good and
the salvation of Mexico, might propose to us
measures calculated to lead to this most desirable end. Your opinion about the present
state of the army, and the future operations of
war, will be accepted by us without hesitation,
and be executed immediately. As we desire

that this serious deliberation might be entirely free, we have resolved that you enter into it without our being present, and charge you to treat this important question conscientiously, and in general, as it is required for the honour of the army and the welfare of Mexico."

His Majesty then retired, and the council of war constituting itself, nominated as president S. E. General Don Miguel Miramon, commander-in-chief of the infantry. The undersigned secretary then took the word, and, complying with the orders of the Emperor, expressed himself in the following manner:

"Gentlemen, there are five opinions here before you, of which H. M. the Emperor has spoken to you. The first proposes a retreat with the whole army, together with our artillery and train; the second will only save the army, but spike the guns, and give up the whole *matériel* of war and means of transportation; the third will continue the defence of the place with the whole army; the fourth proposes to divide the army into two equal parts, of which one should continue the defence of the place, the other to go to Mexico, to bring up from thence reinforcements, in order to compel the enemy to raise the siege; the fifth will charge a small reserve with the safety of the important person of the Emperor, in the case of a disaster, and that one of his generals be appointed to command in chief the whole army, in order to attack the main force of the enemy.

" After having communicated to you these different opinions, of which one is mine, I must explain to the council of war the reasons why I gave it to the Emperor.

" When His Majesty asked me whether we should endeavour to retreat with our whole artillery and train, or give up these two latter, I had the honour to declare to the sovereign that the former proposition appeared to me bad, but the latter still worse, as it would be equal to a defeat prepared by our own hands, by which we would demoralize our army, and thus ruin definitively ourselves and the national cause.

" Should we be placed in the necessity of retreating, and, above all, of spiking our artillery, it seemed to me, as I told His Majesty, to be preferable to leave here a reserve to save the Emperor, and that the army be given to one of our generals, in order to attack the main force of the enemy with all decision. In this case, if a defeat should happen, it would occur only after having tried to save our country and our army, but not appear as an act resolved on and executed by ourselves. I do not believe that we have already arrived at the necessity of giving up the place, as we may still retreat in one manner or the other. There are still provisions and forage for a considerable time; though the state of the park, after a siege of fourteen days, and a valiant defence like that of the 17th, is not so satisfactory as might be desirable, yet it is still better provided than at the time when the enemy appeared in our front, as may be seen from the statement which I submit to the council of war, and which is drawn up with the most scrupulous exactness. For all these reasons, I am of opinion that the defence of the place should be continued, and that in an extreme case the enemy should be attacked with decision, instead of endeavouring to undertake a most dangerous and barren retreat."

General Don Ramon Mendez spoke as follows: "About the difficult question under discussion, I have no opinion of my own, and, therefore, I will subscribe to that of the majority, and do what it resolves."

After him Don Severo Castillo, chief of the second division of infantry, took up the word, and said: "Provided that there is a park sufficient for a certain time, I declare that I do not see any danger, and am of opinion that we should maintain our present position, having in view exclusively its defence, until the moment when we shall be attacked by the enemy, in

which case the same will be repulsed without
doubt. In this case we have to throw our
columns against the Cerro San Gregorio, and,
profiting by the confusion of their retreat, to
endeavour to outflank their position. I do not
judge it prudent to attack the lines of the in-
surgents at the present moment, as, both in
regard to the strong position occupied by the
enemy, and the small number which we could
employ for the purpose of an attack, its success
might be doubtful. However, if this state of
things should be prolonged indefinitely, altered
circumstances must of course alter this decision, as necessity and our best interests may
require."

General Don Saniago Vidaurri, deputy of
the department of war and finance, with His
Majesty, expressed himself in the following
terms: "We must persist in the defensive;
but, at the same time, destroy the force of the
enemy to the left of the Cerro de la Campaña,
and occupy ourselves with the means of extri-
cating ourselves from the present position,
above all, if the present circumstances should
grow worse."

General Don Thomas Mejia, general-in-chief
of the cavalry, declared: "I am for the con-
tinuation of the defence. Should the enemy
offer later an opportunity to defeat them, we

must avail ourselves of it, and, if possible, draw reinforcements from Mexico."

General Don Leonardo Marquez, chief of the general staff, spoke as follows: "I concur in everything with the opinion just expressed."

General Don Miguel Miramon, chief of the infantry, declared: "I also concur with the two last opinions. We shall, however, have to occupy ourselves with the task of defeating the enemy on the roads of Celaya and San Juanico, and, if our present situation should continue, to attack San Gregorio in force."

After the council of war had thus decided to continue the defence of the place, and rejected the idea of giving it up, and had declared against retreating, either with the whole artillery and train, or with spiking the former and giving up the latter, the chief of the general staff proceeded to the apartments of His Majesty the Emperor, to inform him that the council of war had discussed and come to an agreement about the questions submitted to them.

The Emperor thereupon came at once to the place where the council of war was assembled. The sovereign had been meanwhile in great inquietude. The two hours during which the discussion lasted were passed by His Majesty in great anxiety. The undersigned secretary hastened to submit the different points of the present record. From the first opinion which was made known to the Emperor he abandoned himself to a sincere and ever increasing gladness. As soon as he had been informed of the collective opinion of the council of war, the sovereign declared that he accepted with grateful pleasure what had been decided upon. "Our wishes and hopes," he said, "were entirely in accord with your opinion. However—in doubt whether you might not think a retreat convenient, and considering our promise made to you, to accept freely your decision—we passed two hours in real agony. Now we accede not only to the excellent idea of continuing the defence of the place, but also to all inferior points referring to the different opinions.

After a short discussion it was resolved:—

1. To disembarrass the left wing of the Cerro de la Campaña.

2. To put in action the whole force of mounted guerillas against the rear of the enemy.

3. To come to a conclusion in reference to the question, whether reinforcements from Mexico were to be brought up.

4. To resolve on a simple method, proposed by the chief of the general staff, to provide for the pay of the army.

Finally, His Majesty the Emperor declared the council of war as closed, and charged the secretary of the same to draw up the present record, and to have it signed by the generals who formed the council.

> MAXIMILIANO, General-in-chief of the Army.
>
> The General commanding the infantry, MIGUEL MIRAMON.
>
> The General Deputy of the Secretary of War and Finance (vacant).
>
> The General commanding the Cavalry, THOMAS MEJIA.
>
> The General commanding the Second Division of Infantry, SEVERO CASTILLO.
>
> The General commanding the Brigade of Reserve, RAMON MENDEZ.
>
> The Commander-in-chief and Secretary of the Council, MEN. R. ARELLANO.

It will be seen that Vidaurri and Marquez did not sign. I therefore suppose this record was signed after they had left Querétaro.

On the 21st, General Miramon was informed by his spies, that in the village San Jnanico, a league from Querétaro, reinforcements of artillery, ammunition, arms, and four hundred waggons, with provisions, and several herds of cattle, had arrived.

In consequence of this news, I received orders to be with the Cazadores and Tiradores, and my battery, at the Cerro Campaña, next morning, at five o'clock, and to take Juanico. The whole cavalry, under Mejia, was to protect my right, and the cavalry regiment of Quiroga my left flank.

On the 22nd, we were accordingly ready at dawn. The Cazadores constituted the advanced guard, the battery was taken in the middle, and the Tiradores marched in the rear. We advanced on the road to Celaya, which leads directly to Juanico. The road is planted with trees, and to its right is the Rio Blanca. At a distance of about ten minutes from the village we met the outposts of the enemy, whom we followed close on their heels. The infantry at the entrance of the village retired precipitately, and we pursued them to an open place, where they made some resistance. But we did not give them time to form; I called out, " *Viva il Emperador!*" and the Cazadores rushed upon them with their bayonets.

Major Pitner and myself were at their head. I rode, on that day, not my piebald horse, but a little stallion, which was struck by a bullet in his head, and fell on his knees, but recovered directly, and went on again. The enemy did not like cold steel, and fled to the large Hacienda de Juanico, at the end of the village, the headquarters of the commanding Liberal officer.

The regiment Quiroga, which protected my left flank, and marched outside the village, was somewhat ahead of my column, and arrived before us at the hacienda. It made a good charge against the cavalry standing there; and at the same time Mejia advanced on the open plain to my right. The enemy did not show much resistance, and retired to the woods behind the hacienda, which latter we entered. Here we took possession of the office of the commanding officer, with all its papers, and amongst them a statement of the whole army before Querétaro. But, to our great regret, the artillery and greatest part of the provisions had been distributed already amongst the army, and we captured only twenty-four waggons with corn, a great quantity of arms, and many oxen, cows, goats, and sheep.

At our right stood about eight thousand men of the enemy's cavalry, against whom I opened fire with my battery, placed near the hacienda. Whilst we collected our booty, protected on our left flank by the regiment Quiroga, and on our right by the Tiradores, Mejia's cavalry stood opposite that of the enemy, at a short distance, but neither of the parties felt inclined to attack.

As our expedition had succeeded as well as could be, I commenced my retreat, remaining in the rear with the Cazadores. Where a bridge leads over a brook which crosses the road of Celaya, I halted, in order to protect the retreat of Mejia, who crossed the Rio Blanca at a ford to my right. At the same time, my battery, which was placed at the other side of the bridge, and also the artillery from the Cerro de la Campaña kept the enemy at a respectful distance. When I passed the bridge with the Cazadores, I met General Miramon, who cheered the battalion and their leader.

At the Cerro de la Campaña we found the Emperor, who thanked his Zouaves of Mexico, and I rode—it was between noon and one o'clock p.m.—to the above-mentioned coffee-house, where a skilful German veterinary surgeon cut the bullet out of my horse's head. It had entered in an oblique direction, and struck over the eye of the animal.

In consequence of the council of war on 20th March, the Emperor had resolved that Marquez, who was made lieutenant-general of the empire, should go to Mexico, to bring from there all troops he could collect, and as much money as possible, to Querétaro. He was expressly forbidden to undertake any *coup de main* or other expedition, but was bound to return as soon as possible. *Before all the generals assembled, Marquez gave his word of honour to return to Querétaro within a fortnight, coûte que coûte!* With Marquez was to go General Vidaurri, who had been appointed secretary of war and finance, with the presidency in the Cabinet. Both were to be escorted by the excellent regiments Quiroga and No. 5—together, one thousand one hundred horse.

On the 23rd, shortly after midnight, Marquez and Vidaurri started with their staff and escort, marched between the Cerro Cimatario and El Jacal, over the hills, and taking the road over Tuluca, arrived safely in Mexico. In the place of Marquez, the Emperor made General Castillo adjutant-general of the army, and deputy secretary of war in the field. His division was given to my former brigadier-general, Valdez. The march of General Marquez produced great excitement in the enemy's camp, for it was said that the Emperor had gone with him, and a large cavalry force was sent after them, as we learned, a few days later.

This day the Liberals were considerably reinforced by the Generals Riva Palacio, Martinez, and Carebajal. The latter was not our old acquaintance from Tulancingo, but a general

of division, who had been formerly a chief of
bandits. The army of the Liberals, increased
by them, amounted now to above forty thousand
men, with about seventy to eighty guns; and
ours, diminished by the different engagements,
and by the troops which had left with Marquez,
mustered only six thousand five hundred men,
with forty guns. It was, however, somewhat
recruited by deserters and prisoners, who took
service with the Emperor.

On the evening of the 23rd, we were informed by a man from the hacienda where
Escobedo's headquarters were, and whom the
Liberals had made furious by taking everything
he possessed, that there had been held in the
afternoon a council of war, at which was resolved, by a majority of two-thirds, to make a
very energetic attack next morning, as it was
supposed that the troops which had left with
the Emperor must have very much weakened
the garrison. Unfortunately, the man could
not tell anything of the dispositions made for
this attack.

On the 24th, early in the morning, the signal
officer on duty on the tower of the cruz, reported the enemy in force moving with infantry,
cavalry, and artillery from the heights of the
Cuesta China towards the Cerro Cimatario,
where the Liberal columns took up a position.

In consequence of this, I received at ten o'clock a.m., orders from General Mendez to quit my position on the river and to proceed to the Alameda, where I found the Tiradores placed behind the wall enclosing that promenade. Before this wall, in the middle, was planted a battery for three guns, and a fourth stood at the right corner of the Alameda. The Tiradores did not belong any longer to my brigade. Colonel Miramon, who did not like to serve under the command of a foreigner, had managed by the influence of his brother, to have a brigade of two battalions made up for him.

I occupied, with my 2nd battalion of line, the trenches from the corner of the Alameda to the Casa Blanca, where Mendez placed my battery, and remained with the rest of my brigade in the Alameda.

All the batteries of the enemy now opened fire against the city, and at the same time we saw from the movements of the enemy on the hill, that an attack against the right corner of the Alameda was intended.

A column of about six thousand men, under General Martinez, supported by the fire of the batteries, advanced with great resolution. They were newly arrived troops, and had been assured that they would have easy work with us.

As they thus advanced they looked very

well. All of them wore white linen trousers and jackets, with patches of differently-coloured cloth, to show the regiment to which they belonged. In action they looked always uncommonly clean, for it was their habit to wash their clothes before it. As they had only one suit, you might see them stalking about in the camp in a half or entirely Adamite costume, whilst waiting for their clothes to dry.

At the order of General Miramon I debouched with my brigade from the Alameda, passed over a small bridge there, and formed in line to receive the Liberals. We permitted them to advance until they were a hundred and fifty paces from us; but then they received from three sides a tremendous shower of canister and bullets which astonished them so much, that they very promptly faced about.

At the same moment the regiment of the Empress, commanded now by Colonel Don Pedro Gonzales, rushed upon them, made several hundred prisoners, and only retired when the much-scattered column reached the summit of the Cerro Cimatario, where it was protected by the great mass of infantry which had taken up position there. The brown acre before the Alameda was densely covered with dead and wounded, whose white dresses formed a striking contrast with the dark ground.

As dense columns of infantry were seen moving along the Cimatario towards its western slope, it was supposed that they intended a renewed attack against the Garita Pueblito and the Casa Blanca. I therefore received orders from General Mendez to march with my brigade to these places, whilst Colonel Miramon remained in his former position behind the walls of the Alameda.

Without communicating with me, General Miramon withdrew my second battalion from the trenches, where I had ordered them, and relieved them by the Cazadores. I now marched in a parallel direction with the enemy, and when they made front on the broad road which leads down from the western slope of the Cimatario, past the Casa Blanca to the Garita de Pueblito, I made front also. It was now obvious, that the enemy intended to attack us here, and General Mendez gave me orders to defend the Casa Blanca.

This place consisted of a solid stone barn close to the road, and next to the enemy. The space before it was overgrown with cactus plants. Forty paces behind that barn was the Casa Blanca itself, also built of solid stone, and close to it, towards the Alameda was a yard, or corral, surrounded with a stone wall.

I placed the 2nd and 5th battalions of the line

in and near the barn, and in the Casa Blanca;
whilst the battalion Zamora stood at the garita,
where also my battery was placed, in such a
manner as to rake the above-mentioned road
from the hill. The 14th battalion of the line I
kept in reserve, and General Mendez placed at its
side one hundred and twenty horse under Major
Malburg.

After an overture of the artillery by both
parties, the columns of the Liberals commenced
moving at three o'clock p.m. The foremost
column consisted of four thousand men, and
that which followed of six thousand.

The white columns came with great courage
down the broad road, which was not protected
on either side, and permitted our guns from the
Alameda and the garita to pour their shots into
the dense mass of the enemy, which was done
with great precision, especially from the garita,
where General Arellano was himself present.

The composure and bravery of the enemy
under this raking fire, were indeed admirable;
but when their column came up to within four
hundred paces of us, and was overshowered here
by a hail of canister, they began to waver.
They recovered, however, promptly, and advanced two hundred paces more, when to the
fire of our artillery, volley after volley from
our infantry was added. They again wavered,

and we expected to see them turn about. It was a thrilling moment, and comparing our small number with their many thousands, some doubt about the issue might well be permitted.

The enemy stopped, but their officers jumped out in advance of the column; their brave behaviour again encouraged the soldiers; they rushed on in double quick, and succeeded in reaching the barn before the Casa Blanca.

There stood the 2nd battalion of the line under Colonel Madrigal. I rode up to him, and said, "The Casa Blanca must be held under all circumstances, even if we should all be buried here, for with the occupation of this place the city would be lost." The brave colonel answered confidently, "The enemy must yield, or we will all die here."

Although I had much confidence in the bravery of the gallant colonel, I was still afraid that he might have to give up that place, overwhelmed by superior force. My anxiety in that trying moment was so great, that the perspiration rolled down my forehead, and I ordered the reserve to advance.

The place to which the enemy had advanced was not tenable; they had either to go ahead or to retreat. At that critical moment, on which hung the fate of the city, Genera Arellano jumped from his horse, pointed a gun

himself against the densest crowd of the enemy,
and poured into them a hail of canister, which
at this short distance did fearful execution. At
the same moment the brave Major Malburg, with
his detachment of horse, swept round the house
and attacked the enemy on their left flank.

The effect of the canister, and the sudden
attack of the cavalry, whose number was probably over-rated, was too much. The Liberals
were seized with a sudden panic and fled. Now
the battalion Madrigal was not to be checked
any longer. They rushed out from their so
bravely-defended position, and commenced a
dreadful slaughter with their bayonets and the
stocks of their guns, together with Malburg's
cavalry, until a superior force of Liberal cavalry
appeared for the protection of the defeated
column.

Major Malburg captured a standard, and he
and the 2nd battalion made several hundreds
of prisoners. About one thousand five hundred
dead and wounded covered the battle-field,
which looked as if a large flock of sheep were
resting on it. Behind the barn lay, in the foremost line of the dead, ten officers of the enemy,
amongst them the gallant Colonel Mercador,
who led the van of the attacking column.

Our loss was, comparatively speaking, small,
as the Liberal column attacked us with the

bayonet, and even the guns, and the higher standing reserves had to stop their fire when we came to close quarters. General Miramon was present during this engagement, and held the position near the garita.

The enthusiasm of the troops was tremendous when the Emperor appeared on the battleground. He rode up to me and pressed my hand. He had tears in his eyes, and was so deeply agitated that he could not speak; but he whispered three words which made me happier than any decoration whatever could have done—words that will re-echo in my memory and heart until the end of my life. I also was so much affected that I could not utter a single word, but silently kissed that generous hand which rested in mine. Only he who has experienced such moments can understand the feelings produced by them; they are not to be described.

Colonel Miramon remained in the Alameda, and trenches from there to the chapel San Francisquito. My brigade occupied the line to the right from the Alameda until beyond the Garita Pueblito. The other troops remained in their respective positions.

General Mendez had his headquarters in the Casa Blanca, and I occupied the same room with him. This offered me the best opportunity for a nearer acquaintance with this distinguished chief. He, Castillo, Mejia, Escobar, and Valdez belonged to those Mexican generals who were not jealous about the partiality the Emperor showed me; for envy and jealousy are not the exclusive qualities of. the Germans in America, who are noted for it. Whilst the other generals treated me with a certain reserve, those I have named, on the contrary, showed me not only great cordiality, but also regarded with attention my suggestions. Mendez entreated me to induce the Emperor to leave Querétaro, where we could only lose life and honour. In all his conversations he showed a relentless hostility to Miramon.

During the night the enemy had removed some of his wounded nearest to them. When I heard next morning the moaning and cries of the wounded in front of our trenches, I went out with six men to take in as many as possible, and to carry them to our hospitals. When I ventured a little too far, I was nearly captured by ten or twelve horsemen of the enemy, who chased me. I ran through the prickly cactus, as I never did in all my life before, and when I safely arrived inside the trenches, I literally broke down utterly exhausted. As we were fired at when we went out again for the same merciful purpose, we could not but leave the poor

wounded to die a miserable death. Had the
Liberals only evinced the desire to take away
their wounded, we should have assisted them
with all our hearts.

In a day or two the smell from the dead
before us became so intolerable, that I had them
piled up in heaps during the night and burned
by means of wood placed around them. The
enemy, who did not know what we were about,
fired furiously into the burning funeral piles.

In the evening of the 25th March, the
enemy again made one of their usual attacks
against the bridge, and was as usual repulsed.
On that day the Emperor ordered that all the
disposable troops should be employed at the
fortifications. He himself directed the building
of those at the cruz, and exposed himself frequently to the musketry of the enemy. Several
houses on the other side of the river, which
were occupied by the enemy, were destroyed
this day by our artillery.

We were now closely encircled by the lines
of the enemy, who even occupied some parts of
the city, as will be seen on the plan. The
Liberals also took care to strengthen their fortifications, and employed for this purpose about
one thousand Indians, who seemed not to like
their work at all, and whom I frequently saw
run away when our gunshots fell amongst them.

They worked, however, mostly during the night.

The city was every day bombarded, and our trenches were closely watched by sharpshooters, who fired as soon as a head appeared above them. I believe that for this service the one hundred and fifty Americans, who served in the army of the enemy under the name of a " Legion of Honour," and commanded by a Colonel Green, were employed.

Not only the soldiers, but the citizens also, had to undergo many dangers, and the ungallant bullets did not even respect the weaker sex. On the 12th a poor woman was killed by a piece of a shell. Another woman, who carried her baby Mexican fashion on her back, received a bullet through her neck, which killed both mother and child. From the door of my lodging I saw a woman, who had brought her husband his dinner, killed by a bullet. The first thing the unfeeling wretch did was to dive with his hand into the bosom of his poor wife, not to feel whether her heart was still beating, but to secure her money and cigarets, which they always hide in that part of the dress; then he carried the body away without losing time on lamentations, and I even believe that he lighted first a cigaret.

During the night from the 27th to the 28th

of March, skirmishing was going on everywhere along the line. Towards morning the firing ceased, and I had fallen asleep in the trenches. Suddenly, on being shaken at the arm by my aide, I awoke, and still rubbing my eyes, I saw before me the Emperor, with a smiling face. Oh, he had such a kind, benevolent smile, which warmed every heart. In this manner, without an aide or orderly, armed only with his inseparable little glass, he used to visit the trenches during the night or in daytime. As he knew the Mexican officers, and that they not only maltreated their soldiers, but also deprived them of part of their pay and allowances, he was in the habit of asking them whether they had received their pay and rancho. This care had a very good effect, and was so new and flattering to the soldiers that they loved the Emperor for it, especially as he shared with them all dangers and privations. I offered to accompany His Majesty, but he declined in a friendly manner, and continued his dangerous tour of inspection alone.

In the afternoon the Emperor came again, but on horseback, followed by his suite, and the enemy, who must have recognized him, complimented the party with a number of shells.

He dismounted at the Casa Blanca, and sat down in our room with Mendez, smoking a

cigar, which the general offered him.   When he
went away he told me to come every day at two
o'clock p.m. to the cruz to see him, if nothing
particular retained me in the trenches.

The Emperor considered it as a sacred duty
frequently to visit the hospitals, to comfort and
encourage the wounded, and to look that they
were properly taken care of.   As he became
aware that the Mexican surgeons were very
negligent, he appointed his physician, Dr. S.
Basch, inspector-general of all hospitals, and
this gentleman fulfilled his duty with as much
skill as zeal.

When General Marquez left Querétaro he
promised to send news every day, but strange to
say, not one of his messengers had yet arrived;
however, the Emperor was far from suspect-
ing anything wrong from this circumstance.
On the 30th of March, an order of the Emperor
was read, ordering all officers recommended for
decorations to assemble on the Plaza de la Cruz
at four o'clock p. m.   All colonels and subaltern
officers stood there in line, according to their
rank; and before them, also according to their
rank, stood in another line, the Generals Miramon, Castillo, Mejia, Mendez, Arellano, and
Valdez.   By a special order of the Emperor I
had also to take my place in this line.

All the gentlemen in the first line received

the bronze medal for valour, which the Emperor himself attached to the breast of every one, giving him at the same time the Mexican embrazo. When my turn came, and I thanked the Emperor, he said, " Salm, you know how much I am attached to you, and how much I love you. I should like to do more for you, but cannot at the present moment." This related, as he told me afterwards, to his desire of making me general, which he could not do in his present critical position, as it would have occasioned discontent and jealousy amongst the Mexican officers.

The gold and silver medal for valour was given only to non-commissioned officers and privates; the bronze medal could only be received by commissioned officers, and the Emperor was more sparing with this decoration than with any other. The medal, which is worn on a red ribbon, shows on one side the head of the Emperor, and on the reverse a laurel crown, with the inscription inside, *Al merito militar.*

When the other officers in the second line had been decorated also, and the Emperor was going to leave, General Miramon took from Colonel Pradillo, who carried the decorations, a bronze medal, and approaching the Emperor, said, " Your Majesty has decorated your officers and soldiers as an acknowledgment of their bravery, faithfulness, and devotion. In the name of your Majesty's army, I take the liberty of bestowing this token of valour and honour to the bravest of all, who was always at our side in all dangers and hardships, giving us the most august and brilliant example; a distinction which your Majesty deserves before any other man."

The Emperor was much surprised and affected by this ingenious and noble act; he embraced the general, accepted the medal, and wore it from that time as his first and most valued decoration; but whilst all others wore the Emperor's head outside, his medal showed the inscription.

The same evening the Emperor received the following document, very handsomely written on vellum :—

HEADQUARTERS OF QUERETARO,
March 30th, 1867.

" SENOR,—The Mexican army, defending the city of Querétaro, under your immediate command, and which is represented by the subscribed generals, request your Majesty to give them a new token of your generosity, by vouchsafing to ornament your breast with the medal for military merit. Your Majesty rewards, with this honourable decoration, the prominent merit of your generals, chiefs, officers, and soldiers, who

in fulfilment of their sacred duties will endeavour to imitate the heroic courage and extraordinary self-sacrifice with which your Majesty
endures these constant hardships.

" No monarch has ever descended from the
height of his throne under similar circumstances,
to endure with his soldiers, as we here see it,
the greatest dangers, privations, and necessities,
which do not find their equal in the world ; with
soldiers to whom your Majesty understood how
to give such striking examples of self-denying
patriotism and endurance in suffering. Both
the nation, whom your Majesty endeavours to
save and to enhance, and impartial history will
once do justice to the monarch of Mexico—
Maximilian I. The army on their part, relying
on the affection of their monarch, bestow upon
him herewith this medal for military merit.

(Signed)

" Gen. of Division and Chief of Infantry,
" MIG. MIRAMON.

" Gen. of Division and Chief of Cavalry,
" TOM MEJIA.

" Brig.-Gen. and Chief of the General Staff,
"SEVERO DEL CASTILLO.

" Brig.-Gen. and Chief of Second Division of
Infantry, " PEDRO VALDEZ.

" Brig.-Gen. and Chief of First Division of
Infantry, " RAMON MENDEZ.

" Brig.-Gen. and Chief of Artillery,
    " MANUEL ARELLANO.
"The Graduated Gen. and Chief of Engineers,
    " MAR. REYES."

On the morning of the 31st of March I was ordered to go to the Emperor. With him I found two deserters—Alsatians, who formerly served in the Legion Etranger of France. Both belonged to the Liberal artillery, and had arrived before Querétaro only the day before, and their battery was still in the reserve.

The Emperor requested me to examine these two men, and write down what they said, which I did in his presence. They said, as most deserters did, and of which I was convinced later by my own observations, that the soldiers of the Liberals were not only treated by their officers in a brutal manner, but that they also, instead of the promised real a-day, received only a medio perhaps once or twice in a week, and that all their food consisted of corn, to make tortillas, and of frigolio (red beans). Before an engagement they generally received a real and a glass of liquor each. They also said that the chiefs were always quarrelling with each other, which is, however, nothing more than an old Mexican vice.

One of the Alsatians, whose name was Muth

(courage), was a tall, powerful, and very intelligent man. About the position of the batteries on the Cerro San Gregorio he could, however, give no information; but wishing to enter our army and to win our good will, he offered to return to the Liberal camp and endeavour to find everything we desired. He promised to return to Querétaro at twelve o'clock that night. As he was known to none amongst the troops on San Gregorio, he might easily loiter there about under the pretext of collecting wood.

The Emperor seemed to distrust this proposition; but I represented to him that the worst which could happen would be, that the man did not return, for what he could tell the enemy about our city was very well known to them outside by their spies in the city.

The Emperor consenting, I gave this man five piastres, told him that I accepted his proposition, but would retain his comrade as a hostage, and have him shot, if he did not return until noon next day. The Emperor smilingly whispered into my ear, " But which we certainly will not do."

I now led the man myself to our foremost works, and ordered the astonished soldiers not to fire on him when he should return from his mission, either in the day or in the night.

I remained in the cruz, and ordered to report to me at once if anything particular should happen. At about half-past nine p.m., my Alsatian was brought before me by a patrol, and reported as follows :—

He had not been able to run over the whole San Gregorio, as his loitering about had begun to excite a dangerous suspicion, but he had seen on the eastern end of the hill two batteries, behind solid stone works, protected by infantry standing on the northern slope of the hill; and furthermore, that two mountain guns were placed in an advanced position close to the chapel San Trinidad. He offered, if I desired it, to lead me through the gardens of the suburb San Luis, to the place before the church San Sebastian, and thence to the chapel San Trinidad and the San Gregorio.

On this news, the Emperor resolved to attack this position during the following night, in order to take at least the two advanced guns. To this end he sent for Miramon, whilst I returned to the Casa Blanca, taking with me the courageous Alsatian.

Next morning, at two o'clock, I was awakened, and received from General Miramon the order to be with the Cazadores, in the Calle Miraflores, at three o'clock, to report myself to Valdez, and wait for him.

When I reported myself therefore to Valdez

he ordered the battalion of the municipal guards of Mexico, under Colonel Don Joaquin Rodriguez, to join me, as also fifty men of the battalion Celaya, who were quartered in the Meson Sebastian, and knew well the ground around.

General Miramon came at four o'clock a.m., and we then entered a room, where he, by help of a map of the country, explained his plan, which was modified according to my suggestions, and then he gave me the following instructions :—

He was to command the sally himself. I was to go from the open place opposite the bridge through the gardens behind the houses to the place before the church San Sebastian, which was occupied by the Liberals. Without taking any notice of the proceedings of the enemy behind me, I was to advance to the chapel San Trinidad and take it, together with the two guns there. This done, I was directed to storm the two batteries on Cerro San Gregorio, and then sweep its ridge (he spoke French, and used the expression "*balayer*"). He promised to follow with a brigade and to support me, and that another brigade should chase the enemy from the suburb San Luis.

General Miramon seemed to be very fond of giving instructions for such nightly adventures. Some days previously, he had ordered me to be with my Cazadores in the Calle Miraflores at midnight, for a moonshine reconnaissance. I was on the spot, and waited until three o'clock a.m., and as the moon had set about this time, I sent to ask what I was to do. He or his aides had, however, overslept themselves, which had already occurred before. Miramon's aides were very severely reprimanded by the Emperor.

When I passed the bridge, I saw that the troops for my support were ready behind me. As we had to pass through houses and gardens, our servants had orders to lead the horses of the field-officers and aides behind the reserve brigade until they should be wanted.

Without creating an alarm, we came through houses and gardens to the place before the church San Sebastian, and I formed there as silently as possible my troops for the attack. The Cazadores and the fifty men of Celaya were at the head of the column under Major Pitner, and I followed with the municipal guard.

Scarcely had we finished forming before we were discovered at last, and received fire from the church San Sebastian. But as we were not to take any notice of what might occur behind us, we commenced running up the hill. The Liberal company placed near the chapel San Trinidad fled in dismay, and the two guns which they were placed there to guard, had not even time to fire. Major Pitner himself was at once at one, and Captain Maier, of the first company, a Tyrolean, at the other. We captured, with the guns, their ammunition and horses, and some baggage besides. I sent all that directly to the rear, and granted my soldiers a few minutes' rest, as they were out of breath from the hard run up hill.

Our attack, so far behind the front line of the enemy, came quite unexpectedly upon them, especially to General Adrillon, commanding there, and quartered in the chapel, together with Colonel Villanueva, of Escobedo's staff. Both these officers were in bed, and had to run for their lives through the prickly cactus plants, barefooted and in their shirts.

Whilst I was forming my men for the attack against the higher batteries, and day dawning, I saw two Cazadores drag a woman along, who defended herself vehemently. I made my blade dance on the backs of these miscreants, and chased them to their places in the ranks. The poor woman was so delighted with her deliverance, that she repeatedly embraced me; but I am sorry to say I do not even know whether she was old or young, ugly or handsome.

Our servants with our horses had been able to follow our column, and we were very glad to have them. After a short but necessary delay, we stormed San Gregorio. Major Pitner was in advance, with one company of the Cazadores, but arriving on the crest of the hill, he was checked in his rush by a greeting of canister, and the fire of two battalions, placed there in readiness for our reception. The major himself escaped with a deep flesh-wound in the fleshy part of the arm, and the loss of a waistcoat-button, torn off by a bullet; but his men suffered much from this heavy fire. They had to give way, and, pushed towards the right by an overwhelming number, they were separated from me.

Under these circumstances, Major Pitner thought it best to retreat down the hill, in which he succeeded, after a great deal of trouble. The major, a rather stout young man, regretted very much that his horse had not come also, for this running up and down the hill was too much for his fat constitution. He was utterly exhausted, and would have fallen into the hands of the enemy, had not his good luck led to his finding a Liberal mule, which saved him. Without any other impediment, he reached, with the rest of his company, the river, which he forded.

General Miramon, who had promised to follow me, was with his brigade still on the place before the bridge, and skirmishing with the enemy between us. As he did not make a resolute charge, he of course could not follow me.

Though it was now bright daylight, and the Liberals perfectly prepared, and though I did not see the promised reserve behind me, I determined at least to try to fulfil Miramon's instruction, to " sweep " San Gregorio.

I therefore made the attempt to carry the batteries, but the enemy which received us there was so strong, and his position so advantageous, and his fire so murderous, that *we* were swept down the hill, until the chapel De la Cruz del Cerro, the position of which, at the outskirts of the suburb San Luis, I described on another occasion.

Not seeing anything of our reserve, and surrounded everywhere by superior masses of the enemy, to whom the bright day betrayed our numerical weakness, I thought it best to think of a retreat before the enemy's dispositions made it impossible.

To this end I marched in a western direction, to reach the street leading from the height to the place before the bridge; the same in which the rifled gun was placed which we took on the 14th of March. On my way there, I had to sustain a heavy fire on my left flank from the houses at the end of the suburb, and when I turned in the street, I received the fire in front.

It was now certain that I was in a rather dangerous position, which might become fatal, and I think my longing for the arrival of the reserve was very natural. To hasten this, I sent my aide to Miramon, but he soon returned, and told me it was beyond possibility to reach the general, as all the passages were barred. The enemy followed him on his heels, and I received fire from all four sides. Under these circumstances nothing was left me to do but to enter the street, and to rush through it as fast as possible.

The first obstacle we met with was a breastwork. This was taken, and we rushed on. When we passed a cross street, we received fire from both sides, and saw before us another barricade. There was no help ; we received now fire from all sides, and the second breastwork had to be stormed also, and was stormed. All these breastworks across streets were constructed in a manner so as to leave open a passage for one man abreast. That at the first barrier was wide enough to let me pass with my horse, but, at the second, this was an impossibility, and I had to dismount. The courageous Alsatian, Muth, and my servant, were always close by me, and the latter reached past my breast to take the bridle of my stallion, when his arm was struck by a bullet, which otherwise would have entered my breast. I gave my horse up as lost, but the brave fellow succeeded in saving it, and joined me again at the bridge. On the open place before it I at last met Miramon, with the two captured guns. He smiled at me very graciously, but did not say one word why he had left me in the lurch.

Under the protection of troops placed along the opposite bank of the river, and the guns there, we passed the bridge, pressed hard by dense masses of the enemy, who tried to enter with us into the city, but without success. The fight here lasted until noon; I remained with my combined brigade, and returned with my Cazadores to the Casa Blanca only next morning.

It is true, we had taken two guns, but they were rather dearly paid for. We could not think of carrying with us our dead and wounded, who were barbarously murdered. The Liberals in a house opposite, which reached to the river, attached a lasso to the neck of the corpses, and let them down into the river, singing out to us, " There are your cabrones." The brave Alsatian, Muth, who had never left me during the whole expedition, was made a corporal in the Cazadores.

Had Miramon followed with the two other brigades, as he intended to do, we should have taken the whole San Gregorio. The Mexicans cannot resist a vigorous attack; but that was just the thing which Miramon did not attempt, as he commanded only Mexicans, and not the Cazadores, whose impetuosity and wild cries no enemy in Mexico could resist.

The Liberal general whom we had disturbed in his slumbers was removed from his command. The colonel of Escobedo's staff, whom I saw later, told me that not one of my men would have returned if I had stopped ten minutes longer in the street with the two barricades.

ON the afternoon of the 3rd of April, I was called to the Emperor. He had received bad news, which were doubly disagreeable, as in two days the time was up when Marquez had promised to return. Not a single messenger from him had arrived, and that was the more astonishing, as Marquez was more than anybody else in a position to send news, as he could depend on all priests between Mexico and Querétaro. The Emperor began to entertain suspicions of Marquez, but whenever any words to that effect escaped him, he checked himself, and said, "No, no; it is impossible!"

Our provisions, as well as our ammunition, now began to run short, and the Emperor could not but admit that our position grew more and more embarrassing.

To get news from Marquez seemed to be the most essential thing, and I was ordered by the Emperor to consult with General Mendez how to manage this. To this end we had to buy spies at high prices, and Mendez found a woman, an Indian, and an officer. The latter, if successful, was to be promoted and decorated, the two others were to receive considerable rewards. None of them returned, and we never heard their fate.

During the night from the 4th to the 5th April, the enemy again made one of his useless attacks against the bridge. The Emperor visited the trenches quite alone, and, in the afternoon of the 5th, I accompanied him on a ride along our lines.

The 5th of April was the latest day Marquez had fixed for his return, and we had had no tidings of him whatever. In the city, however, a report was circulated that he had been beaten, but as this could not be traced to any reliable source, it was considered to be an invention of the enemies of our cause in Querétaro.

On the 8th April there was great excitement on the cruz, for it had been noticed that masses of the enemy's troops moved over the Cuesta China and towards Celaya, and it was believed that Marquez was approaching; but this was unfortunately not the case.

Under these circumstances a council of war was held on the 2nd of April, in which various propositions were made. One of them was to break through with the whole army; but this was opposed by Mendez, who said, as reliable as his troops were in an action, he could not be answerable for them in a dangerous retreat. Then all the generals, with the exception of Miramon, proposed that the Emperor alone, with the cavalry, should break through, and go to the Sierra Gorda.

The Sierra Gorda is a wild mountain about eight leagues north-west of Querétaro. It is intersected by passes which are of such a kind as not to permit any army to enter, if they are only defended by a few men. Several Liberal armies, who ventured to enter the Sierra Gorda, had been annihilated there in previous years. This wild country was the cradle of General Mejia; here he was an absolute king, and more popular than any other; every Indian child knew Pap Tomasito, and at his first call every man stood to arms.

In this district the Emperor had still a general (Olvera), with one thousand or one thousand two hundred men, and there he would have been able to remain for months, to wait either for better fortune or to make preparations for reaching the coast : but the Emperor declared it "to be against his honour to leave the army, and that he would rather die than do so." Miramon said that the city could still be held for a long time, and that we could wait for Marquez; and the Emperor was of his opinion,

for Marquez *must* return; and as he might
come at any moment, the Emperor resolved to
make, as soon as possible, an attack against
the Garita de Mexico, and to take and occupy
it, in order that we might be able to support
Marquez at once, if he should come over the
Cuesta China.

At the same time measures were taken to
provide ammunition and provisions, which was
done with tolerable success, as General Castillo
found out some concealed magazines, and
General Arellano manufactured ammunition
with great ingenuity and skill. All the brim-
stone and saltpetre in the city was confiscated,
even that at the chemists' shops. The leaden
roof of the theatre and the bells of the churches
were transformed respectively into bullets and
cannon-balls. Caps were manufactured from
stiff paper in a very neat manner, and they
answered perfectly well as the weather was
always dry.

The quarrels between the Generals Miramon
and Mendez were another source of appre-
hension. Mendez asserted that Miramon did
not mean well by the Emperor, and worked
only for his own ambitious purposes He drew
my attention to the fact that Miramon had
recently removed several officers who were entirely devoted to the Emperor, and replaced

them by persons belonging to his own party.

When, on the 10th, I was on my way to pay a visit to the Emperor, General Mendez asked me suddenly, " Do you really mean honestly by the Emperor ?"

" What a question !" I replied. " Of course I do."

" Well," he continued, " then tell him from me to try to get as fast as possible out of this mousetrap, and to beware of Miramon. I am an Indian, and the Emperor knows the faithfulness and the devotion of the Indians for him. If he orders, I will arrest Miramon. Mejia and myself will bring the Emperor in safety to the Sierra Gorda, where he will have his free will, and may do as he pleases. Should he not follow this advice, he may depend upon it that we shall all be shot."

When I saw the Emperor, I repeated to him literally everything Mendez had told me, but he only replied, " The little stout one takes too gloomy a view of our matters, although I believe he means well."

Not to be obliged to pronounce names in conversation with me, which might be overheard, the Emperor was in the habit of substituting certain sobriquets, of which the meaning was only known to us. Mendez was called the

little stout one; Miramon, the *young general;*
Mejia, the *little black one;* and Castillo, the *honest
one,* etc.

The Emperor told me that he would send
for Miramon, to arrange with him an attack
against the garita; but I had not an idea that,
on the urgent advice of Miramon, it was to
take place on the following morning. But when
I received during the evening an autograph
note from Miramon, containing the order to be
with the Cazadores at the cruz at three o'clock
a.m. next morning, I at once knew for what
purpose this order had been sent me. I
directed the Cazadores to be at once relieved
from the trenches by two companies of the 2nd
of the line, and gave orders for them to be
ready next morning at half-past two.

When I communicated my order to Mendez,
he smiled in a peculiar manner, and said, "Why
always you and the Cazadores?" I could not
help wondering also, and having a suspicion
that Miramon might perhaps be glad to get
rid of me, as he knew my devotion to the
Emperor.

Shortly afterwards came Major Pitner, and
told me that the Cazadores were very much
dissatisfied. They said that they had always
done their duty, and did it still with pleasure;
but could not think it quite fair that they were

always to be used as "food for guns." I answered the major that I could not make such
remonstrances to the Emperor just before an
engagement, but that I would do so later if the
Cazadores would do their duty as usual.

On the 11th of April, at three o'clock a.m.,
I was with the Cazadores in the cruz, where I
reported myself to General Castillo. Immediately after me the Emperor entered, and
Miramon came a little later. Miramon, Castillo,
and myself were seated at a table before a map,
whilst the Emperor walked up and down,
smoking a cigar. Miramon took the word, and
said to me, "You will attack the Garita de
Mexico, take, and hold it. I will give you one
of the best battalions, the 1st of the line, commanded by the gallant Colonel Cevallos. With
the Cazadores as an advanced guard, you will
leave the cruz through the embrasure of the
battery on its left flank, and take the road
leading underneath the aqueduct to the garita.
Near that road, on this side of the aqueduct,
stands a house occupied by the enemy which
you will take. Then you will march against
the Garita de Mexico, and take it by storm. As
far as I know, you will find there four guns
and three battalions of the enemy. Your right
flank will be protected by the regiment Empress under Colonel Gonzales, and the hussars

under Captain Pawlowski, who will march on the road leading directly to the garita."

A look on the map will show every one, even one who does not understand much about military matters, that these dispositions were very faulty. I therefore took the liberty of re-marking to General Miramon, that an attack against four guns and three battalions in a strong position, by two, would be rather a diffi-cult task, and proposed that I should be allowed to advance on the road designated for the cavalry. Infantry forces might cover my left flank by marching on the road there, and the cavalry protect my right, moving on another road which leads to the garita past the Chapel San Francisquito.

General Miramon, however, said that he had no other infantry at his disposal, and that I must follow the instructions given. General Castillo is still alive, and will remember this conversation. Miramon told me to wait until he would give me the word to advance. I placed my troops behind the battery, in the north-east corner of the Plaza de la Cruz, which was occupied only by one thirty-six pounder. After a rather long delay, Miramon came, and we had to go in single file through the em-brasure of the gun. When I, sword in hand, came to it, I saw the Emperor standing there with his elbow leaning on the breastwork. " Salm," he said, " I wish you good luck with all my heart; may God protect you!"

The accent in which he uttered these words will never be forgotten by me. It warmed my heart, and I felt elevated at the idea that my so highly-venerated Emperor took an interest in my person, and was anxious for my life.

When I formed my troops for the attack at the other side of the battery, "Diana" was already sounded in the camp of the enemy, and it was too late to surprise them. I do not know why Miramon kept me waiting so long. Sending a company of the Cazadores in advance, I followed with Colonel Cevallos and Major Pitner, with the rest of the Cazadores, whilst the first battalion of the line brought up the rear.

When we came to the house mentioned in my instructions, we of course received fire from it; but the first company took it after a trifling resistance. To my right was the aqueduct which conveys the water from the eastern slope ' of the Cuesta China to the cruz, but which had been partly destroyed by the enemy in the early days of their arrival. This aqueduct is a magnificent monument of the time of the conquest. It is about one thousand five hundred metres long, and its fine pointed arches reach in many places a height of one hundred and fifty feet. Passing under this aqueduct, on the road leading to the ´garita, we were fired upon from the left hand side, where we saw a very strong loopholed stone wall, belonging to a hacienda, opposite the garita building on the other side of the road. As we had no means of getting over the wall, a most singular kind of fight ensued through the loopholes, which were of the same height from the ground on both sides of the wall. One of the Cazadores lost his gun when he thrust it through a loophole, and our men captured two guns of the enemy in the same manner.

Upon this occasion my Alsatian distinguished himself greatly, and did honour to his name, " Muth " (courage). He poked his bayonet into all the loopholes, and animated by his example, my men fired through the loopholes on the defenders in the interior of the corral.

While occupied in this manner we suddenly received a very heavy fire from the azotea of the garita and the other buildings. The Cazadores, who saw nothing but stone walls before them, and who were not in their usual high spirits, pressed themselves close against the wall, and Major Pitner in vain tried his eloquence to bring them from the spot. I therefore requested Colonel Cevallos to advance with his first company to my right, and seeing that it was done, the Cazadores followed abreast with them. The fire by which they were received was, however, so severe, that they soon came to a halt. Under these circumstances Colonel Cevallos, Major Pitner, and myself jumped before the line to encourage our men, but we were followed only by the Lieutenants La Roche and Alphons Marie of the Cazadores, my aide and shadow, Montecon, Sergeant Count Henry Pototski, Muth, my servant, and about eight or ten men, partly Cazadores, partly from the 1st battalion of the line.

Our little party advanced until we came to a turret at the corner of the hacienda building, which was connected with the loopholed wall. Here Major Pitner fell right before my feet, his blood bespattering my boots; he was shot in his head, but though stunned for a time, he was not fatally wounded.

Whilst the major was carried back by two Cazadores, and I was consulting with Cevallos what was best to be done, one of the enemy stuck his gun through a loophole behind me and aimed at my head, which was only a few inches from the muzzle. Lieutenant Alphons Marie noticed it, and had the presence of mind to collar me at once and throw me down, just at the moment when the shot went off. He certainly saved my life, and was decorated for it by the Emperor on the same day.

As our troops would not advance against so superior a force of the enemy protected by stone walls, which they could not storm, Colonel Cevallos and I resolved, though with a very heavy heart, to retreat, which was done in the most perfect order, under the galling fire of the enemy. During this retreat, Lieutenant La Roche and Count Pototski were severely wounded. A company of the Cazadores, under Captain Avisar, who was killed a few days later, formed our rear-guard. We took all our wounded with us, but left our dead.

When I returned to the cruz I met the Emperor, to whom I expressed my regret that our attack had not been attended by success. He answered kindly, "I am glad that *you* returned at least; I did not believe in a success from the beginning." He told me later that he had been very anxious about me, and when the major was brought in wounded, he at first believed it was me.

The Emperor took me with him to his room and permitted me to express myself without restraint about Miramon. I explained to him the faults of the instruction given by him, and told the Emperor how he had left me in the lurch in my attack on San Gregorio on April 1st.

The Emperor answered, "Well we must temporize now. When I am out of this mouse-trap I will alter everything and make it good." He invited me to dinner, which was also attended by Lopez.

At five o'clock p.m. I accompanied the Emperor on a visit to the hospitals. We went to the bed of young Count Pototski, whose right leg had been taken off by Dr. Basch. The count, who was an extremely handsome young man of nineteen, had taken part in the last Polish insurrection, under Langiewitz, had fled from his country, and entered the Cazadores as private, under an assumed name, which was only discovered at a later period. When the Emperor expressed his regret at his being so badly wounded, a smile of satisfaction lighted up the face of the poor young man, who was very much prostrated by the amputation. The Emperor made him lieutenant, and gave him the cross of the Guadelup, which was only worn by officers. The wounded man first kissed the hand of the Emperor and then the cross. Not-withstanding the utmost care the young count died a few days afterwards, pressing with his dying hand the precious cross against his heart.

During the night from the 11th to the 12th of April, the Emperor again visited the lines, accompanied only by Colonel Lopez. The enemy must have had received fresh ammunition, for they bombarded the cruz with unusual energy next morning, and skirmishes took place along the whole line all day. Provisions now began to get scarce in the city. The poor inhabitants lived almost exclusively on maize, but the troops still regularly received, besides maize and horse or mule meat, coffee, and now and then some liquor. The horses of the cavalry and the mules of the artillery only got half their usual allowances, except the regiment Empress, the hussars, who were considered as a kind of life-guard, and quartered in the Meson de la Cruz close by, and the Mexican body-guard, consisting of the most daring men who had been picked out from amongst all the Mexican cavalry, and commanded by Colonel Campos, a Vidaurri man.

When Campos and I were breakfasting with the Emperor, the servant brought in only half a roast chicken, a small piece of bread, and some dulces, which, with the bread, had been presented to him by the good nuns of San Teresita. The Emperor sent for more, but when he was told that there was no more, he said smilingly, " Well, gentlemen, this breakfast shall count for nothing ; come to dinner." We accordingly went, and had splendid roast mule, which had lain in vinegar.

This scarcity of provisions was not the only cause for uneasiness; a greater cause still were the quarrels between General Miramon and Mendez. Each of them insisted that the Emperor should arrest the other, and I was afraid that the Emperor would be prejudiced against Mendez, who seemed to me far more important than Miramon. He had brought the Emperor his best troops, whilst Miramon brought nothing but his person, after having lost his army by his own indiscretion. It is perfectly true Mendez was very devoted to the Emperor, and would have given his life for him, but I was afraid that he, in a sudden fit of anger (to which Indians are subjected now and then), would leave us with his troops, who worshipped him.

The Emperor went to visit him on the 13th, in the afternoon. When he came before the Casa Blanca, and was just lifting his leg over the saddle to dismount, and we had gone out to receive him, a shell burst right over his head. He and all of us could not help saluting the noisy guest with a slight nod, which caused much laughter. This time the soldiers' wives were disappointed, as the shell burst, for whenever a shell reached us they ran to secure it, in hope that it might not burst, as was frequently the case, in order to bring it to the cruz and get the stipulated price for it.

On the 15th the Emperor was closeted all the morning with General Castillo. The result of their consultation was the resolution to send General Mejia with a detachment of cavalry in search of Marquez; but as Mejia was sick in bed and utterly unable to mount a horse, the Emperor resolved to send me. Miramon had to be consulted of course, and he proposed for this expedition General Don Pantaleon Moret, who was his personal friend. General Moret was an agreeable, handsome, fair-haired young gentleman, but nothing of a soldier. The Emperor did not like this substitution at all, but would not contradict Miramon, and after much talking over the matter it was resolved that both of us should go. However, a new difficulty now arose. Who was to take the command? I was a full colonel in the regular army; Moret was only lieutenant-colonel and titular general. The whole business was very annoying to the Emperor, but I assured him that I considered only the importance of the mission, and should be satisfied with any arrangement. The result was the decision that we should be co-ordinate, and " go hand in hand" as the Emperor expressed himself. Moret was simply instructed to find General Marquez in Mexico, or wherever he might happen to be, and to return with him and his troops to Querétaro; but probably he received secret instructions from Miramon. I was officially charged with the same task, but received besides the following secret instructions, which the Emperor dictated to Dr. Basch :—

    1. Three points for the diplomatic corps—

        a. Invitation to some of the gentlemen to accompany Marquez.

        b. To induce the Juarists to proceed in a humane manner.

        c. To make known that the Emperor would not give in voluntarily, if he could not render his commission into the hands of a legal Congress.

    2. Letter to Minister Murphy . . . . *

    3. To communicate only to Marquez and Vidaurri the true state of things, and that we were compelled to eat horseflesh for the last six days.

    4. To give the public good news.

    5. Order to General Marquez *to place his whole cavalry* at the disposal of the Prince.

    6. Prince Salm must demand from General Marquez a decisive answer within twenty-four hours. If he should not obtain it, *the prince is to leave with the whole cavalry after twenty-four hours.*

---

  * These dots here and elsewhere stand in lieu of orders, which I cannot publish without endangering some persons still living.

7. If Prince Salm goes off with the cavalry, he must bring with him at least two hundred thousand pesos and the private money of the Emperor.

8. To send couriers with as much news as possible, and pay one thousand pesos to each.

9. Prince Salm is to spread the intelligence in Mexico that all the generals had desired the Emperor to leave Querétaro with the whole of the cavalry.

10. Prince Salm will influence the Mexican and foreign press. Prince Salm will bring with him all the members of the Boletin de Noticias . . . .

11. Mexico is to be given up altogether, if there are troops enough to relieve Querétaro, but not enough to leave a garrison in Mexico.

12. Papers, both Mexican and foreign, the former from the 20th of February, and slips of the latter to commence on 1st of January.

13. Prince Salm will bring with him all ready civil and military medals, the Guadelup medals, a few decorations, and ribbon for orders and medals.

14. Prince Salm to arrange with Pater Fischer or Vidaurri secret funds for the payment of secret messengers.

15. Prince Salm to bring with him some

good historical or other books according to the selection of Baron Magnus.

16. Prince Salm will bring especially a copy of the pamphlet of Counsellor of State Martinez, and one of the volumes containing the speeches and writings of the Emperor, printed at the office of the secretary.

17. Prince Salm will not forget to ask General Marquez what news he has from General Negreto.

18. Prince Salm to transmit either to Marquez or Vidaurri confidential letters with instructions relating to General O'Horan.

19. Prince Salm is authorized to enter into negociations with persons of the opposite party . . . .

20. Prince Salm will inform himself about the yacht.

Amongst the papers which were taken from me later, and which I therefore cannot give verbally, were the following :—

1. Authorization to arrest Marquez if I should find that the reports about his treason had any foundation.

2. Authorization to arrest General Don Pantaleon Moret, if I should think it convenient.

3. Letter to Colonel Count Khevenhüller in which the same is directed to follow, with his

European troops, my instructions, just as if coming from the Emperor himself, without taking notice of any other orders from any one else.

4. Order to General Olvera in the Sierra Gorda to give me all his cavalry.

In a word I was charged to return with the troops, with or without Marquez, and to relieve Querétaro.

The four letters to General Marquez were the following :—

QUERETARO, *April 16th,* 1867.

" *The Emperor to General Marquez.*

"My Dear General Marquez,—The Prince Salm-Salm is going to the capital to consult with you and other persons about objects of the utmost importance. We therefore recommend you to consider everything he will communicate to you as a transmission of my demands, which you will execute in the manner he will tell you; and at the same time to take care that the same be done by other persons to whom the prince might address himself.

" Your affectionate,

" (Signed)   MAXIMILIANO."

QUERETARO, HEADQUARTERS IN THE CRUZ,
April 17th, 1867.

" *The Emperor to General Marquez.*

" We have given to Prince Salm the strictest instructions that if you, for reasons unknown here, should not be inclined to declare within twenty-four hours, whether you can march on Querétaro with sufficient troops to relieve the city, he is to return here after twenty-four hours; and in this case it is our firm will, and we give the express orders for it, that all regular and irregular cavalry in Mexico and in its suburbs, or on the road between Mexico and Queretaro, *shall be placed at the exclusive disposal of Prince Salm,* who, accompanied by all these troops and General Moret, will directly return here, and as fast as possible.

" Yours, etc.,

" (Signed)   MAXIMILIANO."

QUERETARO, HEADQUARTERS IN THE CRUZ
April 16th, 1867.

" *The Emperor to General Marquez.*

" My dear General Marquez,—In case that Prince Salm is to return alone with the cavalry, you will deliver to him two hundred thousand pesos in order that he may transmit them to us.

" Yours, etc.,

" (Signed)   MAXIMILIANO."

QUERETARO, *April 17th,* 1867.

" *The Emperor to General Marquez.*

" To General Marquez,—In case that Prince Salm on his return here *should not desire to take General Moret back with him,* you will give the latter, on our order, a temporary employment in Mexico.

"Yours, etc.,

" (Signed) MAXIMILIANO."

The 16th and 17th of April passed with the writing of these important authorizations, and with other preparations. The hussars had been increased by volunteers from fifty to one hundred men, and the Espladores de Valley de Mexico, under Captain Don Antonio Gonzales, were to go with me. In order to have my brave Alsatian, Muth, with me, I had him transferred to the hussars. Beside my shadow Lieutenant Montecon, brave Major Malburg, and Lieutenant Bieleck, were to accompany me as aides, and also a German merchant, Mr. Schwesinger, an Imperialist, who desired to leave Querétaro, and who had rendered until then very acceptable voluntary services in the hospitals. I had orders to be at the Cerro de la Campana at midnight, and if everything went right we might expect to reach the Sierra Gorda early in the morning. It was bright moonlight at that time, which was not favourable at all to a secret expedition, yet without it it would have been impossible to find our way over the works of the enemy, which enclosed us.

I took my leave of the Emperor at nine o'clock. He gave me his hand, and said, "Salm, I confide to you much, but I feel perfectly happy in the conviction that I have placed my confidence in good hands." I felt very sad at leaving the Emperor, surrounded as he was with all kind of dangers; but the commission he gave me promised salvation, and I could not but do my best to respond to his wishes.

After taking supper at a French coffee-house, with the officers of my staff, I went at half-past eleven to the Cerro de la Campana, where I already found the regiment Empress and the 4th of cavalry, under Colonel de là Cruz, who were to assist in our undertaking. In a tent standing there I found Miramon in company with General Moret, Colonel de la Cruz, and Colonel Don Pedro Gonzales. The regiment Empress was to follow me, and the 4th to cover my left flank. At the same time infantry was to advance to our right and left on the roads running there.

After an embrazo Miramon left with the colonels, and I remained with Moret, to whom the Emperor had inculcated in the afternoon

that he must go hand in hand with me. When
arranging our march, I expressed the desire to
march with my troops in the advanced guard,
but Moret requested me to leave it to his Mexicans, who had been for the greater part guerillas,
and who were acquainted with every inch of the
ground. As his reasons were plausible, I agreed
to follow him with my hussars.

As soon as we should have passed the river
we were to put the spurs to our horses, and ride
on without taking any notice what occurred behind us. Should we be separated, by some accident, we were to meet at a certain road behind
the village Santa Rosa, at the foot of the Sierra
Gorda. From here we should endeavour to find
General Olvera, and act in concert with him.

The moon shone brightly as we started.
Turning round the Cerro de la Campana, we
came to the river. It was rather deep, and its
banks were steep. We had to pass one by one,
and much time was thus lost. During our crossing we noticed in the camp of the enemy signal
rockets, which indicated the direction of our
march, and arriving at the opposite bank, we
heard to our left and right firing of infantry,
which astonished us the more, as the enemy
generally guarded this plain with cavalry only.
It had the appearance as if the enemy had information of our plan, and I believe now what

I did not then believe, that we were betrayed by Lopez, to whom the Emperor confided things which he ought not have communicated to any others but the persons to whom it concerned.

Instead of advancing at a gallop, we went on slowly, and kept on going thus for about ten minutes, when we received fire in front and from both flanks, on which occasion I got a grazing shot in my leg, and my horse one at its croup. Instead of dashing onwards we came to a dead stop, and I sent Major Malburg to inquire what was the matter. It was long before he returned, and when he came he told me that dense columns of infantry were immediately before us. I sent him again to Moret with an urgent request to advance by all means, and not to care how many might fall, but Malburg returned again with the request of the general to come to his side.

I found him before a water ditch, but which was no serious impediment, as the sixty men of the advanced guard had passed it. On my asking why he had not followed them, the general said that masses of infantry had come between him and his advanced guard, and prevented it. I saw indeed at a distance of about eighty paces infantry before us, who fired into us. Moret asked what we should do under these circumstances, and whether it would not be better to postpone the undertaking.

I saw that it was now an absolute impossibility to ride through the masses of infantry before us, and regretted very much that I had not remained at the side of the general all the time; for some forty of the sixty men of the advanced guard reached the Sierra Gorda, as I was informed afterwards! Underthese circumstances nothing was left but to think of retreating, for the fire in front and on both our flanks had become still more intense, and at the same time we were fired on by two batteries to our right, which had not been there in the afternoon.

Never in all my life was I so furious and mortified as on this retreat, which was owing to the want of decision of General Moret, and still more to the folly of General Miramon, to encumber me with this man, whose unfitness for such an expedition was very well known to him. General Escobar told me at a later period that before my arrival in the tent, Miramon had reprimanded Moret rather sharply about several previous blunders, exhorted him to behave properly on this occasion, which he gave him, to reestablish his military character. The carelessness of Miramon was unpardonable; for though I do not think very much of him, I cannot discover any other reason for his desire to prevent our success.

I cannot describe the feelings with which I went to the Emperor next morning. When I entered he called out, " I know the whole affair already ! " I tried now to induce the Emperor to let me repeat the attempt on another evening, and assured him that I would not return a second time. He liked the proposition.

On April 19th fifteen officers wrote a letter to General Mejia, in which they gave it as their opinion that there remained nothing to be done but to surrender, and which they most earnestly advised should be done. At the head of these faint-hearted officers stood General Ramirez, Colonel Rubio, and Major Adami. These three were put under arrest the same day, and remained so during the whole siege.

The Emperor became more and more aware of the difficulty of his position, and expressed the desire to have me always with him. He would not let me go to Mexico now, and I received his order to remain thenceforward permanently at head-quarters. He still believed that Marquez was on his way back to Querétaro, and Miramon declared, with the greatest assurance, that Querétaro could be held still for months. Therefore, instead of sending me myself, he gave me orders to find a person who would undertake to make inquiries for Marquez.

To leave the city was not impossible to a brave and discreet man, as was proved by the example of our advanced guard.

For this adventure I knew no man better fitted than my brave Alsatian, Muth, and I made him the proposition. I promised him two thousand pesos if he would transmit a slip of paper, hidden in the soles of his shoes, to General Marquez, and bring an answer, or at least, reliable news about him. I gave him twenty-five pesos for pocket money, and he went on his perilous expedition during the night of the 20th and the 21st.

Amongst the foreigners in Querétaro, brought there by the chances of war, was a Mr. Wells, a North American. On the road, with a train of waggons and mules, he had the misfortune to meet Mejia, who thought it convenient to take him and his whole concern with him to Querétaro. Mr. Wells was a very clever and agreeable gentleman. Instead of losing his time and temper, and bewailing his fate, he, with true American versatility, accommodated himself to circumstances. To make himself useful, he attached himself to a hospital, and rendered very good services there, and with such a good heart and will that the Emperor thought it proper to acknowledge them by giving Mr. Wells the decoration of the Guadelup order. He was extremely pleased, republican as he was, and wore the decoration during the whole of the siege.

On April 21st I was appointed first aide-de-camp of the Emperor, in the place of Colonel Osmachea, who was transferred to the cavalry, I do not know why. He was extremely devoted, and during the whole fight of the 14th ult. he was on his knees, praying for victory.

On the other side of the river we saw to-day, hanging on a tree, a man, who had attached to his breast a sheet of paper, on which was painted a large B 5, to show that the man who had been hanged was the fifth of our spies which had been captured.

In the course of the night from 21st to 22nd of April, I was awakened by Severo, the Emperor's Mexican body-servant, and ordered to go to his master. I found him already half dressed. He told me that some person whom he did not name had just informed him that Miramon intended to arrest him this very night. "Though I do not believe this for a single moment," said the Emperor, "I think it convenient to take measures against any emergencies."

As the Emperor did not name the person who brought him this information, I did not like to ask his name; but I suppose it was Mendez.

I ordered the hussars to be ready, and watched myself the whole night, which passed, however, without any incident.

In the morning of the 22nd of April the Emperor sent for Miramon, with whom he had a conversation which lasted two hours. I do not know its object; but when I made my morning report, the Emperor said, " I believe, Salm, the young general is faithful after all." In the afternoon a man, who was a relative of a priest in the city, and lived then in the hacienda de Jacal, the head-quarters of the Liberal General Corona, who held the lines opposite those occupied by Mendez, came to the head-quarters. He had overheard a conversation between several generals.

" The generals," he said, " rejoiced very much about the defeat of General Marquez between Puebla and Mexico."

" That's not true," said the Emperor, interrupting him; " for Marquez has nothing to do between Puebla and Mexico.

The man also stated the generals had discussed the question what would be best to be done with "Maximiliano," and whether he should be made prisoner. All agreed that he ought to be shot; but some of them expressed the fear that the government would pardon and send him to the coast.

"Against that," said Corona, "is still a remedy. He may be shot by his escort, like President Commonfort."

On the 23rd I dined with the Emperor, but our fare was so extremely bad that he could not help laughing about it. I told him that I dined much better the day before with Dr. Basch, whose dinner was cooked by his Hungarian servant.

"That bad fellow!" said the Emperor, jokingly; "I shall take that precious servant from him." The thing was arranged, and our dinners afterwards became better.

In those days I dined now and then at the Hôtel de Diligencias, where we, for a piastre, got some roast horse or mule, beans, and tortillas. I generally carried with me a little piece of bread, which was too small to be divided, and for which I was very much envied. The Emperor received every morning some bread from the good nuns of Santa Teresita, and Dr. Basch, Pradillo, Blasio, and I received each a piece.

General Arellano had been busy for two days past with building two batteries in the projecting angles near the pantheon: one directed against the Garita de Mexico, the other against a battery which the enemy had erected on the road close to the aqueduct a few days ago, in order to attack the cruz also from the east side.

My position did not permit me now to visit much in the city; but, at the desire of the Emperor, I frequently saw General Mendez, who was in a very bad humour, and whom I tried to cheer up. I was more frequently in the company of General Castillo, Colonel Don Manuel Guzman, of his staff, Pradillo, and Father Aguerre. Sometimes we had a rubber of whist with Dr. Basch and the Majors Pitner and Malburg. From six to half-past seven o'clock p.m., the Emperor promenaded regularly on the Plaza de la Cruz, and the enemy must have known it; for at that time the Plaza was always shelled, which, however, did not disturb the Emperor in the least. He was much more disturbed by begging women, especially soldiers' wives, who would not be refused, and whoever was in company with the Emperor had to empty his pockets. During one of these promenades I spent in this manner twenty-five dollars.

On the 24th of April, at seven o'clock a.m., General Arellano tried his new batteries against the Garita de Mexico, and evidently with good success, as the enemy's fire was silenced now and then.

The Emperor went into the cupola of the cruz, to observe the effect of our fire. With him, in the confined little room, were Mejia, who was out again for the first time, Miramon, Arellano, Reyes, Moret, Lopez, Pradillo, and I, with my shadow Montecon, the adjutant of Lopez, and a Frenchman, Captain Kuries. The windows of this small room were half closed by adobes.

A twelve-pounder ball entered one of these windows, and struck against the opposite wall, covering us all with dust and lime; but nobody was hurt! The ball remained harmless on the ground, and the Emperor said he would send it to Miramar as a keepsake, and have inscribed on it the names of all present. Miramon, who himself looked like a miller, had a good laugh at me, as I wore for the first time a new uniform, and because I kept to my eye my powdered lorgnette, wondering why I could not see anything.

The firing lasted until ten o'clock a.m., when it was stopped, for reasons of economy.

The head-quarters of General Escobedo, who commanded the forces of the enemy, had been in the valley between San Gregorio and San Pablo—I suppose in the Rancho de Jesus Maria; but since our attack on the San Gregorio, it had been removed to the south-eastern slope of the Cerro de la Cantara.

On the 25th of April, Colonel Leiza, of Castillo's staff, a very amiable, active little gentleman, was struck on the azotea of the cruz by a shell, which shattered both his legs. He would not have Dr. Basch, who offered to amputate them, but preferred a Mexican surgeon, who cut off only one, and in consequence of which operation he died a few days afterwards.

I had on this day a long conversation with General Castillo about our present position, and we agreed to unite our efforts for the purpose of inducing the Emperor to leave Querétaro.

The Emperor agreed to our proposition, but only under the condition to take his whole army with him. He was always troubled by the fear of not having done enough for his military honour, and then he repeated still, "Marquez will come yet."

This hope was taken from him, however, this day by my brave Muth, who returned from his adventure. In the room of the Emperor I wrote down what he said, but as the original has been lost, I can only give the contents of the document.

When Muth, on leaving Querétaro, crept through the cactus thicket, he suddenly encountered the enemy's outposts pointing their guns at him. As escape was impossible, he waved his handkerchief, and reported himself as a

deserter. He abused, of course, all and everything in Querétaro, and was led to the head-
quarters of some general, where he met a
German aide-de-camp, I suppose a German-
American, from the staff of Escobedo, a Captain
Enking, whose acquaintance I had the misfortune to make later, as I shall relate in its proper
place.

Muth was detailed to a battalion which
occupied the Garita de Mexico, and collected
all information which he thought useful to us.
As all his former statements had proved true,
we had no reason to disbelieve what he now
told us.

It was well known in the enemy's camp that
General Marquez had been beaten by Porfirio
Diaz at San Lorenzo, a place between Mexico
and Puebla, on the 8th or 9th of April; that he
had lost all his artillery, and escaped only with
a few " sombreros chicitos," as the hussars were
called by the Mexicans, from their little Hungarian hats—and that he was now besieged in
Mexico.

He also brought the important news of the
fall of Puebla, and that three Imperial generals
and fifty officers had been shot by the Liberals,
which proved unfortunately only too true.

Muth said that the Liberals did not intend to
make a general attack again, as they were con-

fident of getting the city soon, by starving the garrison.

The Emperor asked him what was the meaning of the ringing of all the bells in the suburbs, and the "Diana" in the lines of the enemy, which was heard some days ago. He stated that this was caused by the good news about the victory over Marquez, received on that day.

This reminds me of General Moret, who had the assurance to order the "Diana" to be sounded, on the Cerro de la Campaña, when he returned from the nightly expedition which miscarried by his inefficiency!

I paid Muth one hundred piastres on account, promising him five hundred or six hundred more on account on the 15th of May, but which was prevented, I am sorry to say, by sad and important events.

The news brought by Muth seemed to confirm the Emperor in his decision to break through with the army, and General Castillo was charged with the task of making propositions in writing for the execution of such a plan. He sent for Miramon, and told him of the information received, and his decision in consequence of it, and gave me many orders, which I executed, with the assistance of Mr. Schwesinger, who spoke and wrote Spanish perfectly well, whilst Basch had to write many confidential letters for the Emperor.

On the 26th of April, preparations were made for our breaking through the enemy, which was to take place next morning at five o'clock. Nobody knew our intention except the Emperor, Castillo, Miramon, and myself.

The Emperor ordered me to put his papers and archives in little valises, which the hussars were to take behind their saddles; and the steward of the Emperor was occupied with this work all day in my room, with locked doors.

I was appointed by the Emperor chief of his household, and he placed under my especial command both the hussars and the Mexican body-guard. I forgot to mention that the commander of the hussars, Captain Echegaray, had been transferred to the infantry, and that his command had been given to Captain Pawlowski.

This officer was a very powerful man, who on one occasion greatly astonished the Mexicans. The cavalry fights of the Mexicans were generally the most ridiculous affairs one could see. Both parties halted at a certain distance, and commenced firing at each other, until one party had enough of it and ran away, when the other pursued them with great noise. When the hussars, instead of conforming to this custom, rushed upon the Mexicans sabre in hand, they were utterly shocked at such rude behaviour, and the more so as Captain Pawlowski, who always carried a very heavy regulation sabre, cut down *seven* of them with his own hand before they recovered from their astonishment.

I had to prepare everything for our leaving as secretly as possible ; and the Emperor, who never forgot anything, ordered that every one near him should carry a note-book in his pocket, in order to write down immediately even the most trifling order, to which he very strictly adhered.

To deceive the inhabitants and the enemy, who knew, however, our position better than we did ourselves, all buglers assembled in the afternoon in the Plaza de la Cruz, to sound " Diana,", and at the same time all the bells were ringing—that is, all which had not been transformed yet into cannon-shot.

I was contented and happy that at last we had arrived at a decision, and slept better than I ever did before.

The exact dispositions for the 27th of April were not known to me; but from what I heard, it would seem as if Miramon cared more for inflicting a severe blow on the enemy than to fulfil our chief purpose.

Whilst Miramon attacked the enemy at the foot of the Cimatario, Castillo, who volunteered to do so, was to make a feigned attack against the Garita de Mexico. Should he, however, by chance be able to take it without much sacrifice, he might do so.

The Emperor was to wait in the cruz for the result of Miramon's attack. With him remained the hussars, the body-guard, and the regiment Empress. Everything was packed up, and ready for our departure from Querétaro.

Between five and six o'clock a.m., Castillo and Miramon advanced at the same time; the former on that road which I had desired to take on April 11th, and the latter from the chapel San Francisquito.

With Miramon was the division of General Mendez, who did on that day his utmost, as he had noticed that the Emperor of late had treated him with some coldness. At the head of the attacking column were, as usual, the brave Cazadores, and next to them was the battalion of the municipal guards of Mexico. Cavalry covered their right flank.

The first line of the enemy and a battery were taken on the first assault by Major Pitner. The attack was made with such impetuosity that a panic seized the Liberals, who fled almost without making any stand. In this attack,

Pitner met the Liberal brigade from Morelia, which was commanded by a German, Colonel Charles von Gagern, whose adjutant, Mr. von Gluemer, was taken prisoner.

After our troops were once in the enemy's line, it was easy work to roll it up, as they were flanked and fired in the back. The Liberals fled like a panic-struck flock of sheep. Fifteen guns, seven stands of colours, and five hundred and forty-seven prisoners, including twenty-one officers, a great quantity of ammunition and arms, officers' baggage and provisions, were the result of this short engagement. The strong hacienda de Jacal, the head-quarters of Corona, was also taken. The panic of the Liberals was so great, that many, and amongst them some generals, ran until beyond Celaya, which is four leagues from Querétaro.

Castillo had also good success. He took a battery of six guns; but as the garita itself, and the hacienda opposite it, were like a fort, and built of solid stone, it was not so easy to take it as an earth breastwork.

We had scarcely sustained any loss, and the purpose of our attack was fulfilled most gloriously, and beyond any expectation. Nothing prevented us from leaving the city, as some hours must necessarily pass before Escobedo could send fresh troops from the opposite lines around the city. Whoever knows Mexican warfare, knows also that any return or collecting of beaten troops was not to be apprehended.

Liberal officers told me later, that their army lost, on that day, not less than ten thousand men by desertion, and cavalry was sent after them into the country, to bring back at least some of them. The defeat was so complete, and appeared so decisive, that some of the Liberal generals proposed to raise the siege, and all admitted that it must have been done, if Miramon had at once assisted Castillo, and the Garita de Mexico been taken.

The poor citizens were jubilant. As soon as they became aware of our great success, they rushed into the lines of the enemy, and helped themselves to all victuals they found there. When the Emperor saw that our troops were victorious, he ordered his household to remain prepared, and rode on the battle-field, accompanied by Pradillo, myself, Lopez, and the hussars. The troops received him with tremendous cheering. On all our lines " Diana" was sounded, and all the bells of Querétaro proclaimed our victory to the country around. When we arrived, I saw, with astonishment, that the troops of Miramon retired to the Casa Blanca, though no enemy was before us ; and nothing prevented him from marching up the Cimatario, to occupy the Cuesta China, and to fire from there into the Garita de Mexico—if nothing beside the original purpose was intended.

The Emperor rode along the lines which had been occupied by the enemy, in a lively conversation with Miramon, and visited also the hacienda de Jacal. In this conversation, I suppose, General Miramon tried to persuade the Emperor to give up for the present his intention of leaving Querétaro, and to make another attempt to annihilate the rest of the enemy's forces, as it had been done with such facility on the south side. The eloquence of the young general was the more convincing, as it was supported by such a stupendous success. It was resolved now that Miramon should advance on the right of the Cimatario, sweep the crest of the Cuesta China, cross the river, and attack San Gregorio. Had this plan been carried out immediately after our success, it might, perhaps, have been followed by a still greater one; but hours had passed, during which nothing was done. The Emperor was, however, full of hope, and said to me, " Well, Salm, the young general is good, after all."

It has been stated, at a later period, by a Major von Goerbitz, a German, of Miramon's staff, that it was not this general, but the Emperor himself, who ordered that a second attack should be made. On my questioning him how the major could know what had been transacted privately between the Emperor and Miramon, the major said that the latter had always been in the habit of assembling his staff after a conversation with the Emperor, in order to communicate to them what had been said or resolved upon.

I asked General Escobar, who had been always with Miramon, and he flatly contradicted that this general ever had this extraordinary habit. General Escobar is still living, and ready to repeat now what he then asserted. But if Major von Goerbitz heard Miramon make this statement, then I must suppose that the general said so for some particular purpose; for, from a conversation between him and the Emperor on that subject, at which I was present, it became obvious that the second attack had been proposed by Miramon. I have not misunderstood this conversation, for I asked the Emperor himself, and he said that I had rightly understood the matter.

Formerly, Marquez was the evil spirit of the Emperor; now it was Miramon. The first is a vile traitor; the latter paid with his blood shed at the same time as that of the Emperor; and as long as there are no proofs to the contrary, we will believe that Miramon, though full of personal ambition, was blinded more by his own illusions, and carried away by his lightness, than that he purposely deceived the Emperor, and advised him badly, in order to rise by his fall.

General Escobedo made a better use of the time squandered by Miramon with such culpable carelessness. As soon as he, from his headquarters on the Cantara across the city, saw the broad side of the Cimatario covered with his panic-struck soldiers, he sent his best troops over the river to repair the losses. Amongst these troops was the battalion de Supremos Poderos, the body-guard of Juarez; the brigade of Nueva Leon, under Colonel Palacio; and even Escobedo's own body-guard, the cavalry regiment of the Cazadores de Galeano, who carried eight-shooters, American Spencer rifles.

It was past nine o'clock a.m. Miramon placed two brigades—one to the right, another to the left of the broad way leading from the Casa Blanca up the Cimatario; the same on which the enemy advanced on March 27th. A third brigade followed as a reserve, and the 4th regiment of cavalry, under Colonel de la Cruz, covered the right flank.

Whether Miramon had neglected to obtain information about the movements of the enemy, whether he, in his intoxication produced by his success, had not even thought it necessary to place a look-out on the crest of the Cimatario, I cannot tell; but it is a fact that the reinforcements sent by Escobedo were already near this crest, on the opposite slope of the hill, when our troops commenced ascending it on the other side. By his negligence Miramon had lost the great advantage of position; and another proof of his carelessness was, that the Cazadores went to this new attack with only two or three cartridges in their boxes! The Emperor, excited also by success, and believing now more than ever in the genius of Miramon, advanced with the general.

When our brigades had ascended about two-thirds of the hill, they were received by a tremendous fire from its crest, where Escobedo's troops had arrived. At the same time, the Cazadores de Galeano swept round the left wing of the enemy, and made an attack against our 4th regiment of cavalry, which was routed, and thrown back upon the infantry. Our troops halted. Their intoxication had not been lasting, for their victory had been won too easy. Moreover, they were already tired by their work of the morning, especially by the running up hill to make prisoners.

The fire from the top of the hill, strengthened by that on their flanks from the victorious Cazadores de Galeano, who fired on that occasion fourteen thousand cartridges, as I was informed afterwards, was too much for them, and they began to waver.

At this moment the Emperor drew his sword and stepped out before the front line. Miramon was on his right, I on his left side. But the fire from the heights proved more effective than the eloquence of his encouraging words and his example; our troops made right about face, and the Liberals advanced from their position. The Emperor was beside himself; he would not retire, and remained on the spot where he was, the target for every bullet. That he did not find here a soldier's death is wonderful. The danger became more and more urgent, for the enemy advanced. Miramon and I entreated him in vain to retire; he would remain. At last I laid my hand on his left arm and said, "I implore your majesty not to expose yourself in such a useless manner, you owe it to your army not to throw away your life!" This had the required effect. The Emperor slowly turned about his horse, and walked his horse to the Casa Blanca.

The slope of the hill offered now a spectacle which cut me to the heart. It was covered with our troops flying in disorder, chased by the Cazadores de Galeano, who killed every wounded man. In the short distance from the hill to the Casa Blanca we lost two hundred and fifty men, among them Lieutenant Wols of the Cazadores, who remained on the field wounded in the face. The enemy made a feint to follow us to the city, and advanced at once against the Casa Blanca, which had been occupied in the old manner. General Miramon who was on the azotea of the Casa Blanca, requested the Emperor to join him there, that he might see how the Liberals would run their heads against our walls. Miramon was not mistaken this time. The enemy halted at about two hundred paces, and when a brave attack of the Cazadores de Galeano against our battery between the Garita de Pueblita and Celaya was beaten off, the Liberals contented themselves with re-occnpying the lines which their comrades had lost in the morning.

When I stood with the Emperor and Miramon on the azotea of the Casa Blanca, I asked the latter what measures he had taken for the security of the cruz? He answered, "Up to this moment none whatever." He had forgotten the cruz altogether, and had it depended upon him the Liberals might have taken it without difficulty. It was, however, not left quite unprotected. The regiment Empress

did infantry service, and Mejia, who went to
the cruz, employed those men who came with
the captured guns.   These together with the
stands of colours and prisoners, were placed on
the Plaza de la Cruz.   Amongst the prisoners
was the adjutant of the Liberals, Colonel von
Gagern, a Mr. von Gluemer, once a Prussian
ensign.   When the Emperor asked him whether
he was a German, he answered with a corresponding expression, " I am an American !" *Civis
Romanus sum !*

The Emperor remained closeted with Miramon for more than an hour, and I went to the
room of Castillo who had returned also.   Both
of us were of opinion that notwithstanding the
turn which things had taken, we might still
fulfil the original purpose of our attack, and
that the present moment was even more favourable than would ever occur again.   A breaking
through with our whole army was possible at
any point of the enemy's lines, but especially
in the direction of the Sierra Gorda, as Escobedo had weakened these lines by sending from
there the troops who had repulsed our second
attack, whilst to-morrow, probably, many of the
beaten troops would have recovered from their
panic and returned.

Everything was still packed and ready, and
the two American gentlemen, Mr. Clark and

Mr. Wells, who had entreated me not to leave them behind, waited impatiently for the signal to march. I had not yet received a counter-order, but the long conversation the Emperor had with Miramon made us uneasy, and we were afraid that this sanguine young general would induce him to stay. I therefore feigned some business in the Emperor's room, and on his noticing me I said in German, " Will your majesty grant me the favour of a few words before dismissing the young general ?"

" Well," replied the Emperor, " wait for me in Castillo's room, I shall be there directly."

He soon came.

" Your Majesty," I addressed him, " will you favour me with the permission to speak to you more freely than I would dare under less precarious circumstances ?"

" I wish you to speak always openly and freely with me," said the Emperor, " even under the most prosperous circumstances."

" Well, your Majesty," I continued, " then I implore you to leave this city, where you certainly will meet your death;" and I developed all the reasons and arguments which I had discussed with Castillo, and this general supported me to the utmost.

But all in vain. The Emperor was utterly infatuated with Miramon. He spoke again of his "military honour" which would not permit him to give up the city with all its heavy artillery.

"And then," he exclaimed, "what will become of this unfortunate city, which has been so faithful to us, and of our poor wounded, whom we cannot take with us?"

Though these scruples did honour to the heart of the Emperor, we could not find them convincing. To surrender a fortress, if not compelled by the utmost necessity, or to lose his guns, may be against the honour of a commander or an artillery officer, and it certainly is desirable that such ideas should become articles of creed in an army, but they cannot possibly have force with a sovereign who must be guided by other motives than solely by his military honour. However, the Emperor was not to be moved; he told us that he had arranged for to-morrow another attack against the San Gregorio.

"Well," I exclaimed, "if your Majesty insists on remaining and attacking San Gregorio, I implore you not to delay it but to make it at once, in an hour."

Castillo was of the same opinion, but in vain; that of Miramon prevailed, and I had to give orders to the hussars and body-guard to retire to their quarters. Thus ended the 27th of April, which offered us the last chance of safety.

The attack against San Gregorio proposed for the 28th of April did not take place, partly from scarcity of ammunition, but still more because the Emperor had been inspired by Miramon with such confidence in a fortunate issue, that he imagined a day more or less would not much matter. Marquez was not thought of any more, and whether he came or not was considered now as rather indifferent, for Miramon felt strong enough to conquer without him. To break through was a thing that might be done every day without much difficulty. The enemy remained quiet that day, and we did not disturb them.

Mendez noticed before his lines a woman on horseback, who wore a sombrero ornamented with a plume, and who carried a gun with which she fired furiously at the enemy. I had noticed her already on former occasions. She looked like a soldier's girl. On being examined by General Mendez, she said that her husband had been killed by the Liberals on March 14th, and that she wanted to revenge him. As she had the appearance of a very resolute woman, the General engaged her to go out and endeavour to bring news from Marquez, for which he promised her five hundred pesos.

She returned after a few days, and said that Marquez would be in Querétaro within two or three days, as she had spoken to him at Arroyo Zarco. But on closer examination, she contradicted herself in a very suspicious manner, and it was thought well to imprison her. She was probably .a spy of the enemy, who would have liked to earn, in an easy manner, five hundred Imperial pesos.

We noticed that signals were made from different azoteas in the city, and heard much later, that the enemy had organized a perfect system of espionage in the city. A station of these scouts was close to the cruz in the houses already occupied by the enemy. Even Liberal officers in citizen's dress, had been in the cruz. Of course all this we heard only after the siege.

Our troops had been very much thinned by their many engagements; to such a degree had this reached, that the infantry was no longer sufficient to man the trenches. Those between the Garita de Celaya and the Cerro de la Campaña were therefore occupied by the 4th regiment of cavalry, whose horses had mostly died by starvation. It was wonderful that the Liberals did not attack this position.

The scarcity of maize was not felt less than that of money. Some cavalry regiments and the artillery teams did not receive any rations at all, and had to feed their horses with leaves and chopped brushwood. The soldiers received only half-pay, and the officers scarcely any.

On the 29th of April the Emperor rode with me and Colonel Lopez along the lines. He was not well, and out of humour. I dined with him in company with Colonel Don Joaquin Rodriguez, and tolerably well, thanks to the skill of the cook, who had been taken from the epicurean Dr. Basch.

On the 30th of April Miramon was called to the Emperor, and as the always active General Arellano had replaced the ammunition, it was resolved to attack the Garita de Mexico that day.

On the 1st of May the attack was commenced at six o'clock a.m., by the battery near the Chapel San Francisquito, which fired against the hacienda de Calleja, nearly opposite the chapel in the lines of the enemy, and the fire was so successful that the place was evacuated by the enemy.

The Cazadores and the battalion of the municipal guards, both commanded by Colonel Don Joaquin Rodriguez, and also the battery from San Francis at once entirely occupied it. The latter opened fire against the Garita de Mexico from one side, whilst it was attacked from another

by the batteries of the cruz.   Arellano directed
the bombardment from the pantheon.

At the same time Colonel Rodriguez with
his troops left the hacienda, and advanced
against the garita; and the Emperor and myself, who observed the attack from a nook in the
cruz, saw soldiers, women, horses, and mules
fly through the back gate of the hacienda, near
the garita.   Our success seemed to be secured,
when the tables were turned by an accident.
Colonel Rodriguez, one of the bravest men I
ever knew, was ahead of his troop; but when
about twenty-five paces from the garita he was
hit by two bullets, and fell dead from his horse.

The death of their colonel brought the municipal guards to a stop, then they fell into confusion, and at last to a retreat.   A reserve was
not there, and the acquired advantage could not
be followed up.   The defenders of the garita
recovered their courage, and followed our retreating troops, who took with them the body of
their colonel up to the hacienda de Calleja.   They
then made an attack against the battery there,
but were repulsed by the Cazadores.   It was,
however, considered advisable to give up the
hacienda, and to retreat again to the Chapel San
Francisquito.

Our artillery fire had, however, done good
service; it had destroyed the wall of the corral

belonging to the hacienda near the garita, and also done great damage to the hacienda de Calleja. In this affair the Cazadores had three officers severely wounded, of whom two died. One had a shot in his head, which laid bare his brains; still he lived until the afternoon.

The Liberal colonel who commanded in the garita, Palacios, was a friend of Colonel Rodriguez, with whom he had been in France as a prisoner of war. The death of Rodriguez was deeply regretted by every one, and on the 2nd of May his solemn funeral took place in the church Congregacion, in which were buried all the field-officers who were killed in battle, or died of their wounds during the siege. The Emperor with his whole staff attended the funeral.

The enemy had now received fresh ammunition, and bombarded the city in an unusually lively manner. In the afternoon it was at last resolved to attack the Cerro San Gregorio next morning.

Our means in money and provisions were now almost entirely exhausted, and it was necessary to take measures to provide for them in one way or other. All the inhabitants of the city were therefore taxed according to their means, and every one had to bring his daily quotum to a certain place at six o'clock p.m. The richest man in the city, a merchant of the name of Rubio, had to pay one hundred and fifty pesos a day. Castillo had the superintendence of this affair, and under him Colonels Antonio Diaz and Francesco Redomet were charged with the contributions in money, and a commissioner, Prieto, with those in victuals and forage.

On the 3rd of May the attack against San Gregorio was to take place at five o'clock a.m., but, for reasons which I do not know, it was delayed until seven o'clock, when the Emperor, who was very much annoyed, was just about to countermand it. It, however, took place in two columns, which in the first rush again took the first line of the enemy; but, as usual, there was no reserve, and the advantage thus gained could not be made available. Everything in the cruz was ready for marching, in the event of our being defeated, and the enemy should enter the city.

General Arellano and myself were with the Emperor in the cupola of the cruz, observing the attack. A cannon ball passed between the head of the Emperor and General Arellano, who was slightly wounded in the head and shoulders by a piece of the wall. I stood behind the Emperor, and believing that he was hit I caught him in my arms. An officer who was on the azotea of the cruz was torn to pieces by another ball.

I afterwards accompanied the Emperor to

the Plaze de Armas, where many wounded were carried past us. Amongst them Colonel Cavallos, severely wounded in his knee, and Colonel Sauza, of the battalion Celaya, who died in the afternoon. A soldier of that battalion on passing alone quite by himself, lifted with his left hand his right arm, torn off by a cannon ball, and hanging only by a piece of skin, and showed it to the Emperor, who made the brave fellow a present and recommended him to especial care. The casino, the former headquarters of the Emperor, was arranged now as an hospital for the amputated and very severely wounded.

The Emperor looked out for an officer to convey to General Miramon the order to hold the line which had been taken until he should send him reinforcements. As no officer was at hand I offered to go myself, but the Emperor said, " No, no, Salm; look out for another, I would not that anything happened to you." Captain Baron von Fuerstenwaerther went to Miramon, but it was too late; the conquered line had been already retaken by the enemy.

This was the last attack made on our side. We had made a number of prisoners who were assembled in the yard of the cathedral, and there examined. They said that everything was very satisfactory in the camp of the Liberals, and that Querétaro would have been taken long ago, if the generals had not been quarrelling and jealous of each other. That was, however, not to be wondered at. Many of them were of different parties, and had been enemies all their life long; they were now only temporarily uniting for the termination of the siege.

CAPTURE OF THE CITY BY TREACHERY.

GENERAL MENDEZ now became very much dissatisfied. He declared that all these engagements had been superfluous, as they cost only men without bringing the least advantage. The only thing to be now done was to break through the enemy's lines. He was so much annoyed that he reported himself sick without being so, and moved to a house at the Plaza de Independencia. He and other generals hoped that the Emperor would disengage himself from the influence of the sanguine general, Miramon; and the Emperor still hoped that the general would find some means to annihilate the enemy and to raise the siege. Thus between mutual hopes, never to be fulfilled, time passed away without anything decisive being done, and our position became from day to day more untenable.

On the 4th of May the city was again terribly bombarded; but that was now an every day occurrence. Our troops in the Casa Blanca noticed a very lean ox running towards our lines, and as he had a sheet of paper between his horns, he excited the curiosity of the soldiers. They went out to catch him, and as the enemy did not fire they succeeded. It was a joke of the Liberals; on the paper was written, that they sent us something to eat, that we might fall alive into their hands. Our soldiers sent in return to the compliment an equally lean horse, that they might be able to overtake us when we should cut our way through.

The 5th of May was a holiday with the Liberals, which they celebrated, by order of their government, in memory of the great victory obtained in 1862, on that day over the French, at the Fort Loretto, before Puebla, in consequence of which the latter had to give up that city, to retreat to Orizaba, and to wait there several months for reinforcements from France.

Lying on my field-bed in the afternoon, a cannon ball passing through an adjoining hall and knocking down a pillar therein, struck against the opposite side of the wall, exactly on the spot where my bed stood; but the pillar had fortunately broken the greatest power of the ball, and the wall resisted.

When I sat writing in the Emperor's room, his little King Charles dog, " Baby," on my lap, Lopez entered and whispered something to the Emperor in a corner. Little Baby, friendly with almost everybody, now jumped from my lap and attacked the legs of the colonel with inconceivable fury, and would not be calmed. The Emperor reminded me later of this occurrence.

Towards night great activity was noticed in the enemy's lines, and at half-past eight commenced, in celebration of the day, a most terrific fire from all the batteries. It was indeed a rare and wonderful spectacle, as each projectile showed its fiery line against the dark sky; and the concert made by about a hundred guns, and the bursting of so many shells was not less affecting for nervous people.

The Liberals had been made drunk in hopes that under the influence of liquor they might succeed in their often-tried attack against the bridge. They came on this time with great fury, and advanced till within twenty-five paces from the bridge; but they were then mowed down by bullets and canister, and fled in confusion, leaving a great number of dead on the field.

The Emperor stayed during the bombardment, which lasted until ten o'clock, on the Plaza de la Cruz, and hussars and body-guard were in readiness.

The 6th of May was a day of rest in both camps. Accompanying the Emperor in his usual promenade on the Plaza de la Cruz, he complained bitterly about Marquez, and the quarrels amongst his other generals. The end of all his complaints was, however, " It is only fortunate that we can break through whenever we like." He spoke also about his relations with Europe, and the French and their Emperor were mentioned, but by no means in flattering expressions. The most approving were his remarks about the Crown Prince of Prussia, for whom he had a most particular predilection. He said, if Prussia should have a war with France, he would accompany the Crown Prince, provided that there was not war against Austria.

I paid General Mendez a visit to-day, whom I found at home, not bodily sick but in an awful humour, and he expressed himself in a manner which made me seriously afraid that his words would be followed by corresponding actions. I therefore thought it to be my duty to draw the attention of the Emperor to the subject. This was the sixty-second day of the siege proper.

On May 7th, several officers were promoted on the recommendation of Miramon. I was very much astonished not to see amongst them Major Pitner, who distinguished himself so much at the various actions, whilst much less deserving and younger majors were promoted. I spoke to the Emperor about this injustice, and had the satisfaction to find that Major Pitner was made lieut.-colonel on the same day ; brave Major Malburg got also at last his medal for his splendid behaviour on the 24th March.

On the 8th of May I accompanied the Emperor to the trenches. Near the Chapel de San Francisquito we saw the soldiers cook cactus leaves. The Emperor asked them whether they got their allowance. They answered that they received their correct ration of mule meat, but less maize, coffee, and beans than usual.

Between the chapel and the Alameda, we had, about one hundred and fifty paces before our lines, a small lunette, protecting a mortar. When the Emperor left with me the trenches to go to this lunette, he was at once fired at. " Salm," he said, " remain here and wait for me." " But," I rejoined, " I cannot suffer your Majesty to go alone !" " Yes, yes, I order you to stay here." I therefore remained on the spot where the Emperor left me, on the field between the line and the lunette, until the Emperor returned, who was astonished to find me there, as he wanted me to return behind the breastwork. "Well," I excused myself," your Majesty ordered me to stay *here*, and here I am." He shook his head without saying a word, and walked on. He exposed himself always, and frequently very unnecessarily, but was always very anxious that it should not be done by persons he loved.

On our way home I tried to persuade the Emperor to visit General Mendez, in hopes that this distinction would act well upon the latter; but the Emperor declined, being afraid that it would be against his dignity. I told him, however, that brave Cevallos was lying with Mendez in the same room, and that the brave colonel, who could only survive a few days longer, would be highly gratified by seeing his Emperor once again.

The Emperor made no reply, but going with me to different places until dark, he then went to the house of Mendez. On entering the room, he stepped at once to the bed of Cevallos, and, whilst I took my place at the bedside of Mendez, he spoke some words of comfort to the dying colonel. Then he came to Mendez, asked how he felt himself, and, after a few indifferent words more, as Madame Mendez and other persons were in the room, he said, " I shall send you Colonel Salm, who has something more to communicate to you."

After having seen the Emperor home, I returned to Mendez, whom I found quite delighted with the Emperor's visit; but his delight was still increased, when I told him that the Emperor had at last decided to cut his way out of the city, and asked his opinion about it. Mendez promised to be well next morning, to consult with Mejia, and to acquaint the Emperor with the result.

On the 9th, about noon, Mendez came. His health and good spirits had returned, and we had a long conversation over a bottle of wine. I told him, also, that the Emperor wanted him next day to attend a Council of War, in which was to be decided how this plan was to be carried out.

General Miramon, for a joke, frightened General Escobedo to-day, whose aversion against bullets was known to him, by directing a battery against his headquarters on the slope of La Cantara. It was, indeed, amusing to see the confusion created by our shot, and the hurry with which everybody decamped from the headquarters. But Escobedo did not relish the fun of this joke of the young general, taking it very ill.

In the afternoon I accompanied the Emperor again on his usual promenade in the Plaza de la Cruz, though it was just at that time rather a hot place. The cruz was not only bombarded with shell and shot, but from the houses near the plaza, which were already occupied by the enemy, a lively infantry fire was kept up against any person who dared to show himself.

The Emperor was in a very sad mood to-day. Eight shells burst around him; he heeded them not, and continued his walk, but noticed on a stone bench near the entrance several officers, amongst them Captain von Fuersten-waerther and Dr. Basch, who seemed to coquet a little with the danger. He sent me there to reproach them, but they remained, probably not thinking it proper to go away whilst their Emperor remained amidst a shower of bullets. However, I was again sent to them to order them peremptorily away.

When I returned, the Emperor said, " Salm, I do not send you away, for I know it would mortify you too much. Stay with me."

We continued our walk for about a quarter of an hour. Shells and balls struck near us in disagreeable quantities, but none of them would satisfy the secret longing of the Emperor.

In the evening Colonel Lopez asked permission that the cavalry, under a Lieut.-Colonel Jablonski, might be permitted to occupy a line of the cruz near the pantheon, to relieve the duty of the infantry a little. As the suggestion of the commander of the Cruz seemed to be reasonable, the permission was given.

Jablonski was a Mexican, but probably of Polish descent. He was a particular friend of Lopez, with whom he was very intimate.

On the 11th of May provisions for man and beast were nearly exhausted. Horses and mules did not get any rations at all, and had to be satisfied with what they found on the plazas of the city. The regiment of the Empress and the body-guard still received quarter rations. The horses of the Emperor were kept alive by provisions which Lopez had got somewhere, and I bought for mine old straw beds, of which the contents were chopped.

We still had wine. We had discovered the secret store of a wine merchant, and confiscated it for the benefit of the hospitals, and sent them as much as they required. The rest was sold to officers, and the money employed also for the benefit of the hospitals. In this manner a box of champagne was also acquired for the Imperial cellar.

At noon the Council of War assembled in the room of General Castillo. I remained in the adjoining room of the Emperor, who frequently entered to tell me what the generals said, and to hear my own opinion.

It was resolved to break through the lines of the enemy with the whole of our little army, *which was still possible at any point we chose.* It is true the enemy had encircled us closely with his lines, but his whole army was employed occupying them, without keeping any reserve at his disposal.

To prevent the enemy from becoming aware of our intention too soon, it was resolved to arm three thousand Indians of the city, who were to occupy the lines whilst we evacuated the place. All the guns were to be spiked by Arellano, with the exception of three or four to make a noise. The Indians were also to fire their muskets now and then. Towards morning they were to throw their arms away, and to retire to their houses. This, however, was to be told them only at the last moment; at present they were to be made to believe that they were to defend the lines, whilst we made a vigorous attack.

General Mejia undertook to organise the Indians, who did anything to please their " Pap Tomasito," and to put the required guns in tolerably serviceable condition.

Mendez was very glad, though he told me we might depend on losing half our infantry by desertion, but that we should reach the Sierra Gorda. The troops would not be harmed by the Liberals; they would be mustered in at once with the army, according to Mexican fashion, but the generals would be certainly shot if captured. He requested me, however, not to say anything about it to the Emperor, for fear that it might induce him to give up his plan.

With making preparations for the great event, the 12th and 13th of May passed away. The

Emperor sent me to Mejia to ask how far he had advanced with his Indians. He said that three thousand of them were ready, but not as yet many guns, and he requested, therefore, that the undertaking might be postponed until the night from the 14th to the 15th, to which the Emperor consented.

In the morning of the 14th I accompanied the Emperor to the hospitals. He was much moved, and frequently repeated how much it grieved him to be compelled to leave the wounded behind; but that they might not remain without proper care, he ordered that doctors and nurses should remain behind with them.

That we intended to break through this night was known only to the generals, but at what point was known to no one; as it was to be decided in a Council of War, to be held immediately before the execution of the plan, in order to make treason impossible.

On our way from the hospitals to the cruz, the Emperor told me that he had appointed me general, and given me a decoration, but requested me to keep it for myself until after the evacuation of Querétaro. The Emperor was afraid of the jealousy of some Mexicans, and did not wish to excite it at this moment. He feared this especially of Miramon, who had frequently asked him in vain to make his friend Moret a full general. This general asserts that he had received his commission, notwithstanding what I have stated, but he could not show it. All I know is, that the Emperor once said, " I will not make a general of him." General Moret wears, also, the medal for ,valour, and the Guadelup cross, but I know with certainty that he received none of these decorations from the Emperor.

Mendez came to see me. He was in a very good humour, and promised me to address his troops before we attacked. Since the night of the 10th we had every night from ten to twelve deserters, and at last about one hundred; but a far superior number of Liberals came during the siege into the city. These Liberal deserters were highly satisfied, as they were treated and paid far better than in the Liberal army, where they were also flogged, a mode of punishment which had been abolished in ours.

On the evening of the 14th of May, everything was ready for marching. The small store of maize we still had was distributed amongst the regiment of the Empress, the hussars, the body-guard, and the officers, that they might strengthen themselves by a somewhat sufficient meal. The treasure of the Emperor was divided between Pradillo, Dr. Basch, Campos, Blasio, myself, and Lopez. We had the goldounzes round our waists. Still later in the night came Lopez to Blasio, to fetch the money which was to be confided to him. He was very indignant that nothing was left to him but silver, and resented it as an apparent mark of distrust, which was not in the least intended, as nobody distrusted him.

About eight o'clock p.m., I was sent by the Emperor to Lopez to inquire whether everything was ready. Mr. Schwesinger was with me. We found the colonel at home, and he answered with the most perfect ease that all the orders of the Emperor had been executed. The Council of War assembled at ten o'clock to decide about the place of attack; but Mejia reported that he had only twelve hundred guns ready, and requested another delay of twenty-four hours. None of the generals opposed, and Miramon said "that it was still time enough, and a longer delay would have the good effect of making the enemy more secure and careless." However, the Emperor decided that this must be the last delay, and that we certainly should break through in the night from the 15th to the 16th of May.

After the generals had left, the Emperor sent for Lopez, and decorated him with the medal for valour. Why and for what deeds has remained a mystery to me. When Lopez had gone, the Emperor told me the resolutions of the council, and said, " I know you are not satisfied with this delay."

" Your Majesty," I replied, " I must confess that I am as little satisfied with this delay as I can approve the reasons of the generals. I should think that twelve hundred muskets and four guns were perfectly sufficient for masking our attack by noise."

" Well," said the Emperor, in dismissing me, " one day, more or less, will be no matter. Take care that the hussars and the body-guard remain saddled."

After having attended to this order, I inspected the house, and, not noticing anything, I went to my room in rather a bad humour. To improve it, I sent the Emperor's *valet-de-chambre* for a bottle of champagne, which I emptied with M. Schwesinger, who slept in the same room with me. After this I laid down on my field-bed without undressing, placing my sabre near my head and my revolver under my pillow. When I awoke in the morning of the 15th of May it was still dark; it was about five o'clock a.m. I heard a noise outside, but did not take much notice of it, as it was always somewhat noisy in the house in the morning. I did not suspect any particular disorder, and the less as I had examined the house only a few hours before, and might expect that anything of an alarming character would be reported to me by the guard.

On a sudden Colonel Lopez entered my room, and said, in a very queer and excited manner, " Quick! save the life of the Emperor, the enemy is already in the cruz !" With that he disappeared, without giving any explanation or waiting for a question. When I had buckled on my sword and put my revolver into the belt, the Emperor's steward, Mr. Grill, came and ordered me to his master. When on the point of following him, Dr. Basch entered, and asked what was the matter ?

" We are surprised. I must go to the Emperor. Hurry up, and tell Fuerstenwaerther to order the hussars to mount, and to be ready before the cruz."*

When I came to the Emperor, I found him dressed and perfectly calm. He said, " Salm, we are betrayed ! Go down, and let the hussars and body-guard march out. We will go to the cerro, and see how we can arrange the matter. I shall follow you directly."

* Dr. Basch says in his book " saddle," but that is a mistake, as I had ordered them myself to remain saddled, and I could not know then that Lopez had afterwards ordered them to unsaddle.

I hurried to the Plaza de la Cruz, and was very much astonished at not seeing a single soldier anywhere; even the guard before the Emperor's room had disappeared. Just as still and deserted was the plaza. The company which had to guard the entrance of the cruz had disappeared, and also the detachment of the regiment Empress, which ought to have been there. At last I met Captain Fuersten-waerther, and ordered him to go to the hussars, who were quartered just across the plaza in the Meson de la Cruz, and also to the body-guard, and to bring them here.

Before I reached the entrance of the cruz on my return, I saw, in the nearly dawning light of the morning, that a gun in the battery there had been upset, and that seven or eight soldiers crept cautiously through the embrasure from the outside. Their manner seemed very suspicious, and on looking sharper I thought I recognized the grey uniform of the Supremos Poderes. I now hurried to the cruz, and met the Emperor descending the staircase. He was in his usual dress, but had over it a great coat, as the morning was cool and he was not well. He had buckled on his sword, and carried in each hand a revolver. General Castillo was close behind him. I ran up to the Emperor, who was on the seventh step from the bottom of the staircase, took his pistols to carry them, and in my excitement, taking hold of his left arm, I called out, "Your Majesty, this is the latest moment; the enemy is there!"

When we stepped out of the door to go over the plaza to the quarters of the hussars, we were stopped by soldiers of the enemy. Involuntarily I raised one of the Emperor's revolvers, but he made a gesture with his hand, and I dropped it. At the same moment Lopez stepped from amongst the enemy, and at his side was the Liberal colonel, Don José Rincon Gallardo. The latter recognized the Emperor, but turned to his soldiers, and said, "*Que passen, son paisanos*" (May pass, they are citizens). The soldiers stepped aside, and we passed—the Emperor, Castillo, Pradillo, and myself in full uniform, and Secretary Blasio.

It was obvious that it was not intended to capture the Emperor, but to give him time to escape. The whole proceeding was so astonishing and striking, that I looked inquiringly up to the face of the Emperor. He understood my look, and said, "You see, it never does any harm to do good. It is true, you find amongst twenty people nineteen ungrateful; but still, now and then, one grateful. I have just now had an instance of it. The officer who let us

pass has a sister,* who was frequently with the
Empress, and who has done much good to her.
Do good, Salm, whenever you have an oppor-
tunity."

Dawn now broke. When we passed the
meson the hussars were not yet ready. Pradillo was sent to tell them that the Emperor
would wait for them on the Plaza de Independencia. On going there, we were followed by
two men of the body-guard, and Castillo entreated the Emperor to mount one of their
horses and ride to the cerro; but he refused,
and sent one of the men to Miramon, the other
to Mejia, with orders to come with as many
troops as possible to the Cerro de la Campaña.

A moment afterwards Lopez came on horseback and armed. He entreated the Emperor
to go to the house of M. Rubio, the banker,
where he would be perfectly safe ; but he was
answered, "I do not hide myself." Lopez
turned round and rode back. On a sudden, as
if risen from the ground, the Emperor's piebald,
in the hands of his groom, stood there. I suppose he was brought by Lopez himself, who
obviously did not wish to include the liberty
and life of the Emperor in his treason.

Strange that none of us suspected Lopez to
be a traitor, though we had all seen him at the

* Or mother; I have forgotten which.

side of the Liberal colonel, and he was free now!

The Emperor waited for the hussars, but they did not arrive; but, instead of them, we saw coming round the corner a battalion of the enemy, and amongst the officers riding at their head we saw Lopez again. Castillo and I implored the Emperor to mount; but he refused, saying, "If you, gentlemen, walk, I will walk also."

When the Liberal officers at the head of the battalion recognized the Emperor, they shortened their steps, and we walked along the Calle de Hospital, through the western suburb, to the cerro.

At the foot of the hill the strength of poor, delicate Castillo was exhausted. The Emperor took one of his arms within his and I the other, and thus we dragged him between us up the cerro, which was occupied only by one battalion. It was now bright daylight, and a most beautiful morning. Suddenly we heard the bells from the cruz give the agreed signal that the vile treason had been successful, and the "Diana" in all the lines of the enemy answered the bells exultingly.

We had scarcely arrived on the cerro when the batteries from the San Gregorio and Casa Blanca opened fire against us. When dense masses of infantry advanced towards the latter, we saw our troops go over to the enemy.

Soon after us came Mejia and Colonel Campos, with a part of the body-guard and several mounted officers, amongst them my faithful shadow, Lieutenant Montecon, Lieut.-Colonel Count Pachta, who was once in the Austrian army, my chief d'escadron, and who died, on his return to Europe, of the yellow fever, Lieut.-Colonel Pitner, and other officers, who would have served the Emperor better if they had remained with their troops.

The Emperor sent for Miramon—but he was out with his staff—to assemble as many troops as possible. In one of the streets he was unexpectedly attacked by a detachment of Liberal cavalry, and shot by the officer commanding it, in his face. The bullet entered his right cheek, and came out near his ear. He was carried to the house of a certain Dr. Licea, an old acquaintance of his, who betrayed him to the enemy the same afternoon.

The anxiety with which the Emperor and we all looked towards the city may be imagined. We hoped to see some of our troops arrive; but, instead of them, came news that several battalions had gone over to the enemy. At last the Emperor saw debouching from the suburb some cavalry in red uniforms, and, with tears, he called out, "Look, Salm, there come my faithful hussars." But this was a mistake; it was only a detachment of a regiment of the Empress, who also wore red jackets. The hussars had followed us immediately; but on entering a street, they saw before them the battalion which we met at the Plaza Independencia. Between this and the Plaza de Armas they were stopped and summoned to surrender by the traitor Lopez. They were compelled to dismount, and were disarmed, with their two brave officers, Pawlowski and Koehlig. The old hussars were furious, and as they could not do anything else, at least they would not give up their horses. Two hussars shot theirs, and the rest drove the others away. They ran up the street directly to their stable in the meson. When they approached the Plaza de la Cruz, the enemy, who still felt very uneasy, was alarmed, and thinking it an attack, the poor horses were received with a volley.

One of our battalions, however, approached the cerro, but when five hundred paces from it, they turned about face. The Emperor sent an officer to persuade them to do their duty; but the noble commander of the battalion laughed directly in the face of the messenger.

The Emperor asked me to speak to Mejia about the possibility of cutting our way out; but the general declared it to be utterly useless to attempt it.

Our position on the cerro now became very hot. A third battery fired against us from the western plain, and that from the Casa Blanca had advanced to the Garita de Celaya, which was not far from us. The fire was so severe that the battalion which occupied the lines sought shelter in the ditches. The shells bursting to our right and left, frightened poor little " Baby," which had followed its master, and came for help to me. It was lost afterwards, and got into the hands of Colonel Cervantes, the late commander of Querétaro, who refused to sell it to me, and had the bad taste to call it " Imperatrice." I intended to take the little dog to Europe, and to present it to the Arch-duchess Sophia.

In the city scattered musket-firing could be heard. Dense columns of infantry, followed by horse, advanced against the cerro, and the three batteries redoubled their efforts.

" Salm," said the Emperor, " now for a lucky bullet." But that bullet would not come, and the Emperor turned again to Mejia, asking whether it was indeed impossible to break through; but he remained of the opinion that it was impossible. Now the Emperor called Castillo and myself, and asked Mejia for the third time; but the brave and bold chief answered: "We have only a handful of cavalry, and part of that is little reliable. Your Majesty may look around and judge whether there is any chance left. I care but little whether I am killed; but I will not take on me the responsibility of leading your Majesty to certain death."

In addition to the fire from the three batteries, we now received also musket-fire from two sides, and on two places of the cerro the white flag waved already. A longer delay would have been madness, and, submitting to dire necessity, the Emperor sent off Lieut.-Colonel Pradillo, under a white flag, to treat with Escobedo about surrender.

The Emperor, who preserved his composure, drew a parcel of papers from his pocket, and directed them to be burnt in a tent by Blasio and Captain Fuerstenwaerther. What papers these were, the Emperor did not tell me.

Our fire, of course, at once ceased; but that of the enemy lasted at least for ten minutes after the hoisting of the white flag.

Other Liberal battalions came from the city, and the cerro was soon entirely surrounded by them. A detachment now approached, at the head of which was General Echegaray, who advanced alone and very cautiously.

The Emperor prepared to receive him. He placed himself in the centre. To his right stood Mejia and Castillo, to his left myself, and the rest of his officers grouped behind us. The Emperor unbuttoned his great-coat, to show his uniform and orders, and, leaning on his sword, he expected the Liberal general.

General Echegaray approached in a polite manner and bareheaded, addressing the Emperor, " Vuestra Majestad," and declaring him his prisoner.

After a few words, the Emperor desired to see General Escobedo. The horse of the Emperor was brought, and also those of Mejia, who gave one to Castillo. My horses had fallen into the hands of the enemy, and I left the lines to look out for one. I saw there a groom holding the Emperor's tall American grey, which had been ridden always by the Empress. At the same moment a Liberal horseman asked the groom whose horse it was, and the fool answered, " The Emperor's ;" on which the Liberal took it away right under my nose. I tried, unsuccessfully, to unhorse a trumpeter of the regiment Empress, when my faithful Montecon became aware of my need, and offered me his horse. He had done so once in battle, when my own horse was wounded. Then I declined ; but now I accepted it with pleasure, and was soon again at the side of the Emperor.

We rode towards the Garita de Celaya. At the foot of the cerro we saw two Mexican horsemen quarrelling, probably about some plunder. One shot the other in his breast, and a jet of blood gushed from the wound in his back, as the bullet passed clear through his body. "Look; how horrible!" said the Emperor, pointing towards the two. We met a troop of officers on horseback. One of them, who was rather excited, approached the Emperor, and, embracing him, called out, "I greet you, not as Emperor, but as Archduke of Austria, and admire you for your heroic defence." Another officer behaved in a very noisy and brutal manner. He pointed his pistol at the Emperor's face, and that of other officers, and would perhaps have lived to immortalize himself with infamy by shooting Maximilian, had not Escobedo threatened to shoot any one who should kill the Emperor, if he should fall into the hands of the Liberals. It served his purpose better to take him alive.

In the neighbourhood of the garita we met Escobedo, with his staff and his body-guard, the Cazadores de Galeano. We now halted, and a ring was soon formed round the Emperor. I was crowded off from him, but he noticed my absence, and called me to his side. We now turned our horses, and rode back to the cerro.

I saw Escobedo here for the first time. He is a man of about forty, of middle height, dark hair and beard, and very dark complexion. He wears spectacles, and has remarkably large ears, which stand off on both sides. He is very friendly after the Mexican fashion, but his face has a treacherous expression. He had been formerly a muleteer, then studied the law superficially, and joined the Liberal party, for which he organized some bands. He had the good luck to surprise an Austrian column, which was escorting a good sum of money, at San Gertrudis, and got some political influence. He is no soldier at all, and careful not to expose his body to fire.

On our way Escobedo was at the side of the Emperor. General Mirafuentes, of his staff, requested the latter, in the name of his general, to deliver up his sword. Another general took mine, and the revolvers of the Emperor, which I had placed in my belt.

On the cerro we dismounted. Escobedo invited the Emperor to enter a tent standing there, and I followed, as Escobedo had also an officer with him—I believe Mirafuentes. Besides us four, nobody was a witness to the conversation ensuing. After the Emperor had been standing a few moments before Escobedo, and the latter remained silent, the Emperor said: "If more blood must be spilled, take only mine." This and two other requests were made by the Emperor; first, in order to spare his army; and, secondly, to enable all persons belonging to his house, and who wished it, to get to the coast, for the purpose of embarking for Europe. Escobedo replied that he would report to his government, but *that the Emperor and those belonging to him should be treated as prisoners of war.*

Officers of the staff of Escobedo have denied this, and it is possible that the general will deny it also, in order to escape the reproach that he broke his word; but I assert, on my word of honour, and am ready to swear to it in the most sacred manner, that Escobedo said what is her estated. I neither misheard nor misunderstood him, for the Emperor referred very frequently to this promise, and an error is therefore not possible.

The Emperor was then delivered to the care of General Riva Palacios, a noted chief of party. I do not know in what relation he may have stood with the Emperor, but the Emperor always made much of him, and had given especial orders to treat him well if he should fall into our hands. The general behaved extremely well, and, as this is an exception, it ought to be especially mentioned. We were to return to the cruz, and the general had the tact not to lead us across the city.

We were escorted by the Cazadores de Galeano. One of their officers, a German-American, of the name of Enking, addressed me. He said that he knew me in North America, where he had been a first lieutenant of artillery, but I did not recollect him at all. He told me, moreover, that my wife had arrived before Querétaro a fortnight ago, and requested permission to enter the city. As her request was refused, she had gone to San Luis Potosi to obtain this permission from Juarez, which could not be refused under present circumstances, and I therefore might expect her arrival soon. This as well as other German officers serving in the Liberal army told me in this way details about the treason of Lopez; but they were blamed for doing so, and prevented by their comrades.

When we came on the Plaza de la Cruz, we found there part of our brave Cazadores as prisoners. When they saw the Emperor they uncovered, and looked on him with an expression of deep sorrow, and many of these old soldiers wept.

At the entrance of the cruz we dismounted,

and the Emperor presented General Riva Palacios with his horse and saddle. The Emperor was then brought to his old room, which, however, like all the rooms, was entirely cleared out. In the Emperor's room, indeed, nothing was left but his field-bed—of which the mattress was cut in search for money—a table, and one chair. Part of the stolen things, amongst them the silver washing toilet—as basin, pitcher, etc.—and many papers, were found in the room of Lopez. The anger expressed by this fellow the night before, when he found silver instead of gold was confided to him, is quite sufficient to characterize him.

Many officers of the Liberals crowded the room to see "Maximiliano de Habsburgo," whom they could not conquer otherwise than by treason. Amongst them were Colonels José (Peppi) Rincon Gallardo, and his brother. The former is the same officer who said in the morning the " *Que passen*." Speaking to the Emperor about the treason of Lopez, he said: "People like him are made use of, but then kicked." In the corridor before the Emperor's room stood a company of the Supremos Poderes, and a sentinel before his door. On a flat, balcony-like roof, opposite the door, at the other end of the room, stood another detachment of soldiers.

Pradillo, Count Pachta, Blasio, and myself, were taken to a room which was entered from that flat roof, so that, on going over it, we could communicate with the Emperor. Later, Dr. Basch joined us. The Emperor embraced him. Mejia and Castillo were quartered in the room of the latter. It was ten o'clock a.m. when we re-entered the cruz.

The health of the Emperor had suffered by bad food and other circumstances; he had not been well before, and went to bed. He was, however, visited by a Liberal general, whose name I did not hear: he sat down at his bedside, and asked the Emperor many questions about Mexico and Vera Cruz, which he answered in his open manner. As he spoke a great deal too much, and I feared he might tell many things which it was not necessary that the enemy should know, I placed myself behind the chair of the general, and laid my finger on my lips. The Emperor understood, and soon broke off the conversation.

We were all very hungry, as we had not eaten anything since last night. Senor Rubio sent the Emperor a slight dinner towards evening; but he ate only a few bits, and we divided the rest amongst us.

The other officers—about four hundred—were quartered in the church of the cruz, where they were much annoyed by Liberal officers, who came to stare at them. Lieut.-Colonel Pitner and Major Malburg joked about a sentinel at their door, whose thin, hungry figure and ragged state amused them. Colonel Doria, a man known in the Liberal army as a bloodhound, noticed it, and said: "Laugh on, gentlemen; these fellows are still good enough to shoot you." This observation damped a little the merriment of these officers. The command over the cruz and the prisoners was given to General Don Pansho Velez.

IMPRISONMENT OF THE EMPEROR.

In the morning of the 15th, we were awakened already before five o'clock, by furious drumming in the yard below, where the soldiers had done all they could to make a noise during the night. I looked down, and saw a Liberal officer with a drum hanging round his neck, and beating it like a madman, at the same time animating his soldiers to support his efforts by more noise.

Amongst the soldiers I noticed some Mexicans of our Cazadores, who were already mustered into the Liberal army. The foreigners, however, were not trusted, and locked up.

This day, was published the following army order of Escobedo :—

Mariano Escobedo, Division-General the Mexican Republic, General-in-Chief of the Northern army, and commanding the troops operating around Querétaro.

"Soldiers,—The Republic owes to your valour, constancy, and sufferings, one of its triumphs, the greatest it has obtained in the great struggle of the nation against the invaders and their accomplices. The rebel city of Querétaro, the strongest fortress of the empire, has succumbed, after an heroic resistance, worthy of a better cause. Ferdinand Maximilian, the titular Emperor, Miramon, Mejia, Castillo, and a large number of generals, commanders, and officers, together with the whole garrison, are our prisoners. I should fail in my duty as a soldier, and commit treason against my conscience as a free man and loyal Mexican, were I not to speak of your heroic deeds and your sacrifices. With the faithfulness of soldiers, who defend the independence of their country, without provisions, and frequently, without even a cartridge, you looked upon the face of death without flinching, opposing the numerous troops of the traitors and foreigners, who were excellently provided with every kind of war material, excellently fortified, and commanded by the best generals of our former army, who, unfortunately, forgot their duty in joining the intruders, and supporting, to the last moment, the foreigners whom another foreigner, the Emperor of the French, placed on a throne erected by the bayonets of his soldiers. But these soldiers are no more here; the remainder of them have flown to France, to hide their disgrace, loaded with the curses of a whole people; and the sad news, that more than half their comrades paid for the caprice of their ruler with blood.

"Companions in arms! It does not matter whether ambitious, ill-disposed persons, try to disparage your heroic deeds, veracious history will put every one to his proper place; and neither the enemies of the Republic, nor those who remained in the places occupied by the invaders, looking with indifference on the misfortune of the country and Republic, will be placed above those who, like you, fought without rest for the sacred principles of independence and liberty.

"Soldiers! With all the devotion of my soul, I congratulate you in the name of the Republic, and the Supreme Government; and, true to the programme which I have made, we will continue to strengthen the hands of peace and order, and with them, the prosperity of our country.

"Viva the Republic! Viva the National Independence!

Headquarters, at la Purisima frente, Queré-taro, May 15, 1867.

"MARIANO ESCOBEDO."

I need not add a single word to this pompous document, which I translate for the amusement of the reader, in order to give them a sample of Escobedo's veracity.

Besides this, the Liberal commander-in-chief published a notification directed to all Imperial, military, and civil officers, to report themselves within twenty-four hours, threatening that every one should be shot without any trial, who should not obey this order within that time.

In consequence of this, Generals Escobar, Casanova, Moret, Valdez, the Minister Aguirre, and some others, reported themselves, and were quartered in the room of Castillo.

The Generals Arellano and Gutierez, and Colonel Don Carlos Miramon, had succeeded in making their escape from Querétaro, and General Mendez, after whom the Liberals were searching most eagerly, was still concealed in the city.

When old General Escobar, after having given himself up, was marched with an escort through the streets, he met there the traitor Lopez, who had always been on bad terms with this honest man. The dastardly traitor had the revolting impudence to give his unarmed enemy a slap in the face.

We saw much marching amongst the Liberal troops in the afternoon, and heard that all those who could possibly be spared, were sent to Porfirio Diaz, who was besieging Mexico.

Escobedo remained in Querétaro, as he was an enemy of Porfirio Diaz, and would not serve under his command. General Don Pansho Velez also was sent to Mexico, and was replaced by General Echegaray, a relation of our major of the same name.

The regiment Empress was left together, and entirely. officered by the Liberals. All these officers were, however, killed afterwards, by their men on a march, and the regiment organized itself into a guerilla band, with the intention of joining some later conservative movement.

General Escobar had made many friends amongst the citizens of Querétaro, and from them he heard everything that happened. He brought us the sad intelligence that forty of our officers had been shot or lanced the day before. The soldiers had placed them, as in joke, against the walls of the corrals, and killed them with shot, or with their lances. Amongst them was Colonel de la Cruz, of the 4th cavalry, and Colonel Campos, who fell into the hands of the enemy when wounded at the cerro, and was immediately despatched.

Towards evening we heard suddenly a peleton fire in the cruz, and Dr. Basch was sent for, from whom we heard the reason. In the church, where so many officers were quartered, a number of cartridges were scattered on the ground. Some of them were ignited by cigars which had been thrown away, and on the noise produced by it, the officers, afraid of an explosion, thronged towards the entrance. The guard, believing that an outbreak was intended, fired upon them. Three of our officers were severely wounded, and one of them was killed. The same fate befell an officer of the Liberals, who was wounded in the abdomen.

The officers of the Liberals with whom we spoke made no secret at all of the treason of Lopez; and it was known amongst them that he had now practised this trade for the third time. The first time was during the war against the United States, under Santa Anna. General Escobar gave me the original of the following document, which General Miramon showed the Emperor when he intended to make Lopez a general :—

GENERAL STAFF OF THE ARMY.
SECTION OF THE ARCHIVES.

[*Circular.*]

His highness the General President orders that the ensign of the active cavalry regiment Monterey, of Neuva Leon, D. Miguel Lopez, shall be dismissed from the army unconditionally and for ever, and this in consequence of his infamous behaviour in Tehuacan, where he seduced the body-guard of his Excellency the President to revolt, commanding in person the troops operating against the army of the United States.

This order will be made known to the army, that the same may learn that if the Supreme Government rewards faithful servants, it also punishes those who are no longer worthy to belong to the honourable profession of soldiers.

By high order, for your and your subordinates' information.

(Signed) QUIJANO.

MEXICO, *June 8th*, 1854.

It is difficult to understand how the Emperor could confide the cruz, and with it his person, to a man with such antecedents. However, I have already remarked, I did not believe Lopez intended to deliver the Emperor into the hands of the Liberals. Afraid of being shot, if captured, he endeavoured to save his life, and earn at the same time a good round sum of money, by giving up the city into the hands of Escobedo. The Emperor frustrated all calculations and arrangements to save him by his refusal to conceal himself in the house of M. Rubio. A fellow like Lopez, without honour, could, of course, not understand that a man, an Emperor, might prefer death to an action which he considered to be, if not against his honour, at least against his dignity.

On the 17th, early in the morning, notice was given to us to prepare to be transferred to the convent Santa Teresita, out of which the poor nuns, whose order had occupied that place for centuries, had been driven. We met, on the Plaza de la Cruz, the other officers. The uncertain fate before us made us all serious, and we embraced our friends in silence. We were escorted by a formidable force. One battalion marched at the head, another brought up the rear, and two companies marched to the right and left along the houses. The Emperor was with Dr. Basch and General Echegaray, in a carriage.

The inhabitants of the city showed much sympathy for us, especially the women, who greeted us with tears. When we arrived at the entrance of Santa Teresita, many women passed through the lines of the guard, and gave the prisoners oranges and cigars. The poor nuns had kept the convent very clean. There was a yard inside, with a vaulted open walk around, and a fountain in the centre.

The Emperor's room was very large, but entirely empty. The same was the case with an adjoining one, where all those persons were

quartered whom the Emperor had desired to
stay near him. There were General Castillo,
Minister Aguirre, Colonel Ormachea, Lieut.-
Colonel Pradillo, Dr. Basch, Blasio, Colonel
Guzman, and myself. We were not, however,
allowed to communicate with the generals who
were in a separate room, or with the other prisoners who were quartered in other parts of the
convent. As we had lost all our things, and
must sleep on the floor, the Emperor ordered
a serape, or Mexican shawl, to be bought for
each of us.

On the 18th of May, a long list of all the
prisoners was published. At its head stood, in
larger print, Emperador Maximiliano, which
was changed, in later issues, to Archduke Ferdinand Maximilian " de Habsburgo." The
health of the Emperor improved; but we lost
General Echegaray, probably because he treated
us too well, and in his place came General
Rufio Gonzales, who had been formerly a chief
of brigands.

We heard absolutely nothing about the intention of the enemy in reference to us, and the
report was circulated that the Liberals were
shooting all foreigners, when I was called out
about eight o'clock p.m. I prepared for the
worst, and my comrades did not expect to see me
again; but it was a false alarm, for the Liberals

only wanted some information about my nation-
ality, and other purely personal matters. In
the yard, twenty-two sentinels were placed,
who, all night long, called to each other at the
top of their voice, "*Sentinella alerta!*" so that
we could not close our eyes.

On the 19th of May, General Escobedo,
accompanied by General Diaz de Leon and
Colonel Villanueva, visited the Emperor. The
visit lasted half an hour, and we were all very
much excited; but this visit was only a for-
mality, and we heard nothing positive. Some
officer of Escobedo's staff told me that my
wife was expected to arrive very soon.

During the previous evening, General Mendez had been captured in a house, betrayed by
his own servant for money. Escobedo was
very glad to apply to him the rule he had made
in his notification, for Mendez would have been
shot under any circumstances, as he had once
ordered two Liberal generals, Arteaga and
Salazar, to be shot. To others who were captured even later, this rule was not applied—at
least, as far as I know.

Next morning I stood with others near the
window, when Mendez was led through the
passage opposite us. He walked fast, as usual,
and smoked a cigar. When he saw us, he
smiled, and waved adieu with his hand. He

was led to the external wall of the Plaza de Toros, near the Alameda, where he was to be shot by a detachment of the Cazadores de Galeano.

It is the custom in Mexico to shoot those from behind who are considered as traitors by the opposing party, into whose hands they fall. Mendez would not submit to this insult, and, when compelled to kneel down with his back towards the guns, he turned round on one knee when the men were about to fire, raised his hat, and called out, " *Viva Mexico !* " He fell on his face, wounded, but not killed, but was perfectly conscious, for he pointed with his index finger behind his ear, requesting in this manner that they would shoot him there, which was complied with by one of the Cazadores. The body was given up to his wife. These details were told me by the officer who commanded at the execution, a former Swiss barber, who had deserted from the French Legion d'Etrangers. He had not forgotten his old trade, and offered to shave me—of course, for a consideration. In the evening, we heard that twelve of our guerilla officers had been separated from the rest, to be shot in the morning; but I could never ascertain whether this was done.

On the 20th of May, about noon, my wife arrived. Her news was by no means comforting, for she said that it was intended to shoot us all. She had a long conversation with the Emperor, in which she gave him much information, especially in reference to the treason of Marquez, which mortified the Emperor far more than that of Lopez.

It was the general opinion that Marquez marched towards Puebla, instead of Querétaro, with the intention of joining Santa Anna. The German officers in Mexico, who wanted to relieve the Emperor, had been always quarrelling with him.

As the Emperor expressed a wish that he might be quartered with his suite in a separate house, my wife went to persuade Escobedo, with whom she had become acquainted, as well as with some officers of his staff, when she had come before Querétaro, to request admittance the city.

On her return, she told us that Escobedo had made some promises to her, and concluded from his conversation that he intended to enter into some negotiations with the Emperor.

This proved correct, for at four o'clock p.m., Colonel Villaneuva, of Escobedo's staff, requested the Emperor to go to the general's head-quarters. The Emperor at first was unwilling to go, but at last he changed his mind, saying, "Well, Escobedo has paid me a visit,

and I may return it; but he did it only upon
the condition that my wife and I should be permitted to accompany him, to which the colonel
did not object.

The Emperor gave his arm to the princess,
and I followed with Colonel Villaneuva. We
passed the other prisoners, and they saluted
the Emperor with great respect and love. We
then stepped into a carriage, and, escorted by
twenty-five men of the Cazadores de Galeano,
we drove to Escobedo's head-quarters, which
were, since the occupation of the city in the
Fabrea and Hacienda de Hercules, belonging to
M. Rubio.

In front of this hacienda is a very large,
fine garden, into which we entered. Near a
basin with a fountain, Escobedo came to meet
the Emperor, and went with him into a large
side-walk, where chairs were placed for the
party. Many curious officers were standing
near the basin, and two bands were playing
alternately.

The Emperor spoke with Escobedo about
his abdication. He asked that his officers
should be brought to the coast, in return for
which he would give orders to surrender
Mexico and Vera Cruz.

Escobedo answered that he would report
this to his government. On his part Colonel

Villaneuva, and I, from the Emperor's, were charged to arrange between us the points mentioned in the conversation, and to write them down.

I spoke for some moments with the Emperor, who gave me his instructions, saying, "Do it in an honourable manner, for I would rather die than degrade myself." He then wrote the following authorization—

QUERETARO, HACIENDA DE HERCULES,
le 20 *Mai*, 1867.

J'autorise mon colonel et aide-de-camp Prince de Salm-Salm de traiter avec M. le Général Escobedo, et je réconnais les actes faites pas le premier comme faites en mon nom.

(Sig.)   MAXIMILIANO.

My negotiations with the Liberal colonel were facilitated by the circumstance of his speaking French very well. We agreed that my propositions in the name of the Emperor should be made in the form of a letter directed to Escobedo. This letter ran as follows—

QUERETARO, HACIENDA DE HERCULES,
le 20 *Mai*, 1867.

Son Excellence M. le Général Escobedo, Commandant-en-Chef des Forces Libereaux.

GENERAL,—Mon Seigneur et Souverain m'ai

autorise de traiter avec vous sur certain points, pour éviter plus d'effusion de sang dans ce pays.

Pour arriver à ce but il vous propose—

1. L'abdication officielle de la couronne du Mexique ;

2. Promesse solemnelle de ne plus jamais se mêler dés affaires politiques du Mexique ;

3. Ordre à ses Généraux-et-Chefs, de mettre bas les armes et de rendre les places fortes ;

4. Ordre au commandant des troupes etrangeres de mettre bas les armes, de se rendre sous la protection des forces Libéraux pour se rendre à Vera Cruz, afin d'être embarqué ;

5. Qu'il recommande le sort de ses généraux et officiers Mexicains, qui lui sont resté fidèle, a la genérosité du nouveau Gouvernement;

6. Qu'il soit escorté a Vera Cruz par une escorte choisie par vous, Général, avec les personnes de son entourage ;

7. Que tous les etrangers qui sont prisonniers ici soient transporté à Vera Cruz, afin d'être embarqué.

J'ai l'honneur d'être, Général, votre devoné,

(Sig.) PRINCE DE SALM-SALM,
Colonel et aide-de-camp de S. M.

Before giving this letter out of my hands,

I showed it to the Emperor, who made some slight alterations, after which it was delivered as above.

The whole negotiation lasted about one hour and a-half, after which we returned in the same manner in which we came to our prison in the convent.

On the 21st of May we heard that twelve *French* officers in the service of the Emperor, who had been employed mostly as paymasters, and who had done no other service during the siege, .had offered their services to General Escobedo. As it would be a pity to bury in oblivion the names of these fellows who had the miserable courage to do such a thing, I will give them here as they were published in the " Sombre de Arteaga," a Liberal Querétaro paper—Captain Ernest de Rozeville, Lieut. Jean Ricot, Captain Charles Schmidt, Captain Henry Morel, Captain Xavier Gaulfreron, Lieut. Félix Kieffers, Lieut. Emile Trouin, Ensign Eugen Bailly, Lieut. Theodore Heraud, Lieut. Emile Pejuin, Lieut. Victor Nomel, and Lieut. Paul Guyon.

Escobedo answered them in a letter couched in very severe and contemptuous expressions. He told them " that the cause of the Liberals could be fought out by themselves, and that he could not accept the services of people who, in the face of their suffering companions, could make such an infamous offer, and from whom a similar behaviour might be expected on a future occasion."

The steps taken by those twelve officers caused a storm of indignation amongst the prisoners; and the other French officers sent me the following letter for the Emperor, which I promised them to publish later, with their names—

Des Français officiers prisonniers, à sa Majesté Maximilien, Empereur du Mexique.

Sire,—Nous avons appris que des Français officiers prisonniers, comme vous, avaient demandé au Général Escobedo la *faveur* de servir dans son armée.

· La feuille Liberale à justement appréciée cet acte le taxant d'infamie, et le Général Escobedo a bien fait de ne pas accepter des hommes qui n'ont pas craint de faire une pareille demande dans de telles circonstances.

Comme ces officiers (qui, pendant tout le siege, n'ont assisté a aucune affaire), sont Français, et que votre Majesté pourrait croire quil ont été les interprêtes de nos sentiments, nous nous empressons, Sire, de rejeter toute, participation à cet acte inqualifiable, qui a soulevé notre indignation.

Nous profitons de cette circonstance, Sire, pour donner à votre Majesté l'assurance de notre entier devouément et que, quoiqu'il puisse arriver, nous nous ne nous avilerons jamais.

Nous sommes, avec le plus profond respect, Sire, votre Majesté les très humbles, et les très fidèles sujets,

A. Page, capitaine; Eugène Chardin, Adolphe Marie, Jean Marc, Jean Baptiste Gobin, Jéronimo Guitard, Charles Bomet, Adolphe Charton, Charles Eloy, Antoine Vignoli, Charles Desprez, Gustave van Haecht, Gaspard Wéry, Henzy Voignier, Eugene Laroche, Fréderic Filliatre, Leopold Dreyssé, Adolphe Chigon, Adolphe Bouzeran, Chrétien Ludwig, Charles Schupbach, Jean Lugeon, Adolphe Sibenaler, Zacharie Deplace, Albert Hans, Henzy Ehrmann, Louis Depain, Jean Baptiste Parison, Ernest Coudray, Jean Nicolas Girardin, Léopold de Potter,—lieutenants.

Of our captured soldiers the Liberals scarcely took any care whatever, as may be seen from the following letter, which I received :—

YOUR HIGHNESS,—In the name of all his imprisoned comrades, the undersigned requests you, for the mercy of God, to represent to his

Majesty the Emperor, our miserable position, that we, as faithful servants of his Majesty, may not be starved to death. Since our capture on the 15th, until now, most of us have eaten scarcely a morsel, so that every one of us already wishes for death in any other manner. We, therefore, beg your Highness to induce his Majesty to favour us graciously with a charitable gift.

IVAN BUDSKY,

Imprisoned hussar, in the name of his comrades.

When my wife came in the afternoon, she had forgotten her pass, and was refused admittance by the officer of the guard in the most rude manner. I was furious at this, and paced the room in a rage. The Emperor, who was just then with us, and was a witness of the scene, pointed smilingly at me, and said to the other gentlemen, "There, look at the lion in the cage."

When returning with her permit, my wife brought for the Emperor and myself some much welcome linen.

On the 22nd of May we were informed that the Emperor, some of his suite, and the generals were to be transferred, not to better quarters, as we had hoped, but to the convent of the Capuchins. The reason of this separation became known to us only later.

Escobedo had received from the " Supreme Government" the order to shoot us all without delay; but he remonstrated, and said that it could not be done without a previous trial, and might involve the government in difficulties with the United States, which had already expressed themselves officially about the proceedings at San Jacinto, highly disapproving of it.

The Emperor was lodged in the pantheon, or grave vault of the convent; the generals were quartered in a large hall, and we in some place adjoining the pantheon. As the Emperor did not feel well, Dr. Basch was sent for at his desire; when the doctor asked me where the Emperor was, I frightened him horribly, without intending to do so, by simply saying, " In the tomb."

In this convent we met Miramon, his head still bandaged. The Emperor embraced him. The latter was to-day visited by the Hamburg Vice-Consul in San Luis Potosi, Mr. Bahnsen.

We were, however, not to stay long in that horrid place, but were transferred on May 23rd to another court, where we had a little more comfort, and three or four persons were quartered in a cell. My wife did not give up her endeavour to get a separate house for the Emperor, but she was put off with promises.

When, on 24th of May, I was sitting with the Emperor in the yard, in the centre of which stood a very large lemon-tree, Colonel Palacios, who under Gonzales, had the especial guard over the prisoners, called me aside and requested me to tell the Emperor to prepare for his removing to a separate room, as his trial was about to commence, he would have to be alone and without communication with the other prisoners. When I had fulfilled this disagreeable duty, the Emperor ordered his steward, Mr. Grill, to pack up his things whilst I walked with him up and down the yard. He remarked, "You see they progress slowly, but securely. It will be soon at an end."

I saw lying on the ground a thorn crown, which had fallen from the head of a wooden image of Christ, which had been used by the soldiers as firewood, and picked it up. The Emperor took it from my hand, and said, "Let me have it, it suits well with my position." He gave the thorny crown to Mr. Grill, and ordered him to hang it up in his room.

The cell in which the Emperor was confined was in an upper story of the convent, as were also those of Miramon and Mejia. Before each of these cells a sentinel was placed. As the

Emperor desired to have Dr. Basch near him, he, Mr. Grill, and the *valet-de-chambre*, Severo, were placed in cells close to those of the Emperor.

From a conversation I had with Colonel Palacios, who had been a prisoner in France, and spoke French tolerably well, I learnt that there was but little hope for the Emperor. In the course of the conversation I remarked that the Mexican Government would do well to take an example from the North American Government in their treatment of the rebels of the South, on which Palacios said, "The North Americans are our born hereditary enemies. We will neither have anything to do with them or with you; we can exist without any of you."

I ridiculed the idea of living quite alone without any connection with other nations, and without any trade, after the example once given by China and Japan, but he sustained his opinion, and said that Mexico produced everything required for her existence, and needed no foreign relations. I endeavoured to induce Colonel Palacios to permit me to communicate with the Emperor, as he before his death would have to make many arrangements. However, it is impossible to get from a Mexican a straightforward answer, and I could get nothing except some vague promises.

When my wife came on the 25th of May, she was in a state of great excitement, for she had heard for certain that the Emperor and myself would be shot, and that the trial of the former had commenced this day. The law of 25th of January, 1862, would be applied, which orders that every one captured in arms should be shot. The whole law proceeding, the execution included, would be finished within three days. At the same time with the Emperor Mejia and Miramon were to be tried, and after them three others, according to their scale of rank. In this manner I was enabled to make the interesting calculation how soon my turn would come.

With some difficulty I was permitted by Palacios to see the Emperor, but only in the presence of the officer of the guard. That officer happened to be my Swiss barber, who, for a consideration, remained standing at the door, watching that nobody disturbed our conversation.

I informed the Emperor of what I had heard from my wife, and we agreed that she should travel to San Luis Potosi to try her luck with Juarez, and obtain, if nothing else, a delay at least, as time is a great deal under such circumstances.

My wife was very busy that day. She came

several times to my prison, and for the last time at eleven o'clock p.m., when she prevailed upon some officer to bring both of us to the Emperor, from whom she received her instructions. From the Emperor she went to Escobedo, to tell him that she was going to see Juarez, and requesting him to postpone the execution until her return, which she would hasten as much as possible. Escobedo promised according to Mexican fashion. She departed the same night.

On 26th May I had a long conversation with Colonel Villanueva, who was an educated man, and not so bloodthirsty as most of his fellow officers. The *resumé* of his conversation was, " Maximilien est perdu," and there was no remedy against it.

I endeavoured to go to the Emperor, and was at last successful. As nothing so much prevents vigorous action as weakly hope, I thought it to be my duty to represent to the Emperor the true state of things. I did this chiefly to win him to an idea which had flitted across my brain all these days—viz., *escape,* which alone promised help.

An officer of the troops occupying the convent, an European, visited me frequently, and smoked a cigar with me. As he was not particularly disagreeable, and I always got news from him, I tolerated his company, and gave him money as often as he applied for it. This officer was to assist me in the escape of the Emperor, and I was almost certain that he would not refuse to do this service.

The Emperor was first horrified at the idea of " running away," but I attacked his prejudice with all the reasons and arguments I could muster. I proved to him that he had done more than sufficient for his " military honour," and that it was a duty he owed the world to preserve his life; that he was only thirty-five years, and a brilliant future was before him, and he might still be of very good service to humanity.

The Emperor was at last persuaded, but bade me consider that I forfeited my own life if such a plan should be discovered. I requested him not to be troubled on my account, as, in the worst case, it was tolerably indifferent whether I was shot a few days sooner or later. When I returned to my room I prepared myself for my Liberal officer with a few bottles of wine and other things, and he soon made his appearance.

I came at once to the point, saying to him: I will speak plainly to you. You are here a lieutenant, and have not been paid for months. You see most of the Mexicans, whether Liberals or Imperialists are blackguards, and you have indeed very little chance here. I will propose something to you, by which you may make your fortune. Assist me in saving the Emperor. As soon as we have passed the gate of the convent, I will give you three thousand piastres (I held the roll of gold right under his nose), and on our arrival in Havana I will pay you a thousand ounces of gold (about four thousand pounds) more; besides care will be taken of your future in Europe.

The officer did not make any other objection, but accepted at once. I then gave him a little note for a personage in Querétaro, whom I informed of my plan, and requested to assist me.

As it was desirable for me to communicate freely with the Emperor, I requested the same to write to the Fiscal about it. He did so, and the Fiscal sent me on the 27th of May the following note :—

" Fiscal,—Puede el pres * Salm hablar con Maximiliano en español y delante del comandante de la guardia, Querétaro, Mayo 27 del 1867.

" Aspirez."

From that time I was almost all day in the room of the Emperor, whither I was accom-

---

* *Pres* means in Mexico not a prisoner of war, but a criminal prisoner.

panied by an officer who took me back also.
Though we were to have spoken Spanish only, it
was sufficient to mix now and then a Spanish word
in the conversation. As the officer's room was
close by and the Emperor's room open, the
former was supposed to be present. We dis-
pensed with his company with pleasure.

The next thing I did was to inform the Emperor of my success with the officer I have
mentioned. The Emperor desired me once to
measure his cell, " for future times ;" therefore I
will describe it as well as its surroundings.

The part of the convent in which we were
imprisoned, was a building enclosing a small,
quadrangular yard. Round three sides of this
yard ran in both stories passages, or open gal-
leries, with stone arches open towards the yard,
which once had been closed with trellis work,
but which was now broken away, and left only
in its upper parts. The fourth side of the yard
was separated from the adjoining similar one by
a wall.

The Emperor was in the upper story. The
doors of the cells opened on the passage with
the arches, and also the windows. The staircase leading to the upper story was in one of
the corners. After ascending it, one had on the
right a cell in which were the captain and lieutenant of the guard; in another were the men ;

at the opposite side was, in the left corner, the
cell of the Emperor; next to it that of Miramon,
and, in the right corner, near the separating
wàll, was the cell of Mejia.

To the left of the staircase were only two
cells; the next was occupied by the Emperor's
steward Grill, and his Mexican *valet-de-chambre*
Severo; the other by Dr. Samuel Basch. The
one long wall of Dr. Basch's cell was separated
from the Emperor's cell by the passage, which
formed thus a kind of niche. Before each of
the doors, always open, of the Emperor and the
two generals, stood a sentinel.

The cell of the Emperor measured six paces
by four. Opposite the window opening stood a
field-bed with a chair at its foot, and a small
mahogany table at its head. On the diagonal
of this square table stood four silver candle-
sticks with wax candles, the only luxury which
the Emperor would not relinquish, and besides
some trifling things lay on it, which were always
arranged in the same convenient order. Acci-
dental disturbance of this order offended the eye
of the Emperor, and was corrected by him immediately. On this table always stood a glass
with sugared water, covered with a card against
the many flies.

In the other corner opposite the door stood
a table, at which I was usually writing. To

the right of it, against the short wall, stood a box of the Emperor's, which had been recovered from the room of Lopez. In the corner opposite the bed, and near the window, was a washstand. As the Emperor did not feel well, he usually remained in bed until noon, and was up only for a few hours.

On the 28th of May the examination of the Emperor came again to a stop, and a lively exchange of telegrams between Escobedo and Juarez took place. When I was sitting at the bedside of the Emperor, he remembered that, though he had appointed me general and promised a decoration, I had not yet received the patents. Though his powers were now at an end, he said he hoped that I might require such documents, and therefore ordered Blasio to make them out from the date of the verbal appointment, viz., May 14th. He made me grand officer of the order of Guadelup. He also made my wife lady of honour of the San Carlos order, which had been instituted by the most excellent Empress Carlotta. He said he would have made her "palastdame" of the Empress, but that it was an impossibility, as the document had to be signed by the Empress herself. General Castillo, Colonel Pradillo, Dr. Basch, and others were also decorated.

As everything was now uncertain, and we

might be separated unexpectedly, the Emperor told me to trust to his *valet-de-chambre*, Severos, who was a true and reliable man. As he carried my breakfast to my room, I might always look whether there was a little note concealed in the bread; but as it might be dangerous if such a note should fall into the hands of the enemy, he dictated me the following numbers as marks for different persons and things :—

1, Emperor; 2, Miramon; 3, Mejia; 4, Salm; 5, the officer of the enemy whom I had won; 6, my wife; 7, another officer of the Liberals; 8, Mexico; 9, Vera Cruz; 10, Tampico; 11, Matamoras; 12, Turpan; 13, horses; 14, ...; 15, Austria; 16, man-of-war; 17, ...; 18, small boats; 19, mules; 20, physician; 21, chiefs of the enemy; 22, Havana; 23, New Orleans; 24, Washington; 25, Liberal government; (26, left out); 27, Marquez.

On the 29th, an officer mounted guard whom I had not hitherto seen, and who was more strict than the rest. I therefore could not speak much with the Emperor, but had enough to arrange in reference to our escape, which was made extremely difficult by the Emperor's positive declaration that he would not fly without Miramon and Mejia. Measures had, therefore, to be taken accordingly.

When the infantry officer, **my** confidant,

came to see me to-day, he said that nothing could be done without the officer of cavalry who commanded the guard near the Emperor's room, and that he had already spoken to one, whom he asked permission to come and see me. Though it seemed to me rather dangerous to take so many persons into our confidence, the thing was done, and I felt glad that this officer of cavalry was one with whom I had been already connected in money matters.

I sent now to my confidant in the city instructions to buy the following necessary things: six horses, six revolvers, and six sabres. For the use of the Emperor, I ordered that my piebald horse should be repurchased, as it was taller than the Mexican horses, and an excellent jumper. All these horses and arms were to be concealed in houses by lady friends. The officer of cavalry, my old acquaintance, was ready enough to save the Emperor and myself, but it was rather difficult to make him agree to the escape of Miramon and Mejia.

On the 30th of May, at breakfast, I found in my bread the following pencil-note of the Emperor, which I have still, framed under glass :—" I require necessarily black thread for binding, beeswax for pasting, and, if possible, a pair of spectacles. On the horse must be fixed two serapes, two revolvers, and a sabre.

Not to forget bread or biscuit, red wine, and chocolate. A riding-whip is also necessary."

The Emperor would not cut off his beautiful beard, but tie it behind the neck, and put on spectacles. He said he would look so ridiculous without a beard if he should be retaken, and had laughed himself very much on seeing General Casanova, who had cut off his enormous moustaches the better to disguise himself, and who could scarely be recognized by his most intimate friends.

I went to see the Emperor, but could not speak much with him until the strict officer was relieved at noon by another whom we already knew. As my cell was on the ground-floor, and those of the Emperor and the two generals upstairs, I should have to pass sentinels on two sides, and the Emperor therefore requested Escobedo to transfer me to the room of Dr. Basch, as he required my assistance in writing down his last will.

The Emperor told me that Lopez had had the impudence to offer his services, but that he had, of course, declined them. The traitor was not satisfied with the Liberals, who had paid him only a small part of the stipulated sum. The Emperor spoke of Lopez, the traitor through cowardice, only with contempt, but of Marquez,

the cold-blooded, calculating traitor, with indignation.

Many people procured from Escobedo permission to see the Emperor; and when my wife
returned, very sad and weary, in the evening,
from San Luis Potosi, some Americans were
with him. One of these visitors described the
scene in a paper, and I will give his description,
as that of an unconcerned eye-witness frequently
conveys a far more correct idea of a situation,
than can possibly be done by one of the interested persons :—

"A bustle was heard outside; the heavy
door was opened, and a soldier announced, 'La
senora!' In an instant Prince Salm-Salm held
the new-comer in his arms. She was the voluntary messenger, his wife, who had just arrived
from San Luis Potosi from Juarez. Her face
was sunburnt and soiled, her shoes were torn,
her whole frame trembled with nerveless fatigue
as she laid her hands upon her husband's
shoulders. The archduke came forward eagerly,
waiting his turn. The prince was heard to ask
in a whisper, 'Have you had any success?
What did Juarez say?'

"'They will do what they have said in the
despatches. They have granted the delay.' She
turned to Maximilian, 'Oh, your Majesty, I am
so glad.'

"Maximilian took the princess's hand, and kissed it. 'May God bless you, madame!' he said, 'you have been too kind to one who is afraid he can never serve you.'

"The princess forced a smile. 'Do not be too sure of that, your Majesty. I shall have some favour to ask for the prince, here, yet.'

"'You will never need to ask that, madam,' responded the archduke, leading the lady to a seat. 'But you look weary. You are very tired. We can offer you little. Prince, you must care for your——. I——'

"Turning his face aside, Maximilian moved abruptly towards the window. It was easy to see why. His grief was restrained, but almost audible. The prince—with one hand on the back of his wife's chair, and with the other uplifted toward the archduke in mute protestation—could hardly restrain his own emotion."

It was time intrusion should cease. The visitor, who had already reached the door, made an unnoticed salute and withdrew.

On May 31st, in the morning, I was sitting at the bedside of the Emperor, when "Jimmy" (perhaps still recollected from Tulancingo), stormed through the door, jumped right on the bed of the Emperor, and was extremely glad to see me again. A bright smile played over the face of the Emperor, when he said, "There, our guardian angel is coming!" for of course the irrepressible Jimmy was followed by his mistress.

At breakfast already I received by the bread-mail the following little note, written by Dr. Basch, from the Emperor :—

"You must cause the Hamburgian Consul Bahnsen to telegraph to the English, Italian, Prussian, Belgian, Spanish, and Austrian legations, that the process against the Emperor has commenced, and that he requires time to arrange urgent and important private business, as also important international affairs between Austria and Belgium, concerning the person of the Empress."

It was now resolved that the princess should go to Mexico and return thence with the Prussian minister, Baron von Magnus, and a lawyer. For the former the Emperor dictated to me the following letter :—

QUERETARO, 31st *May*, 1867.

DEAR BARON VON MAGNUS,—I wish very much to see you, and request you to come here as soon as possible; bring with you the Austrian and Belgian representatives, as I have to arrange with both gentlemen some important family affairs of an international character. I beg to have Colonel Schaffer and Count Khevenhueller; perhaps it **may** be arranged to send off both gentlemen as Prussian or English couriers. Schaffer and Khevenhueller shall wait for me in Havana. Perhaps it might be well to bring also our English representative.

I request you to send my things to Messrs. Will and Co., Prussian Consuls in the Havana.

Your affectionate

(Signed) MAXIMILIAN..

When I had finished the letter the absence of Jimmy was discovered. Where could he be? After much calling he condescended to pop his black nose out of the Emperor's bed, where he —to the horror of my wife—was taking a nap. The Emperor laughed when the free-and-easy American, who does not care either for kings or emperors, resisted his being removed.

The Emperor now spoke about our escape; he said, " The white flag was hoisted, and we surrendered as prisoners of war, and as such Escobedo has acknowledged us, on the Cerro de la Campaña . . . . Juarez has not accepted my conditions, and, instead of considering us as prisoners of war, we are treated as rebels; therefore, we are under no obligations whatever."

It was arranged that we should go first to the Sierra Gorda, and from thence to Tuspan, a place on the coast, from whence the Emperor would reach Vera Cruz, which was still occupied by our forces. He hoped here to obtain better conditions from the Liberals, especially for his subjects that had remained faithful to him.

The Emperor dictated the following instructions, which I copy from my tablets :—

" The Austrian ships in Vera Cruz are to be instructed carefully where they are to cruise (under-score that!). Signals during night and flags in the daytime. Besides this, to send small boats frequently on shore. It would be good to enter into communication with English and Spanish vessels."

For the minister Aguirre, who was with me in the same room downstairs, the Emperor gave the following instructions :—

"Letter to the Austrian and Belgian ministers to come immediately, to treat with them family affairs of an international character. Minister Aguirre has to sign."

After I had left the Emperor, I had a visit from my Liberal officer who told me that his comrade of the cavalry would mount the guard near the staircase on the 2nd of June, and that he himself would command the infantry guard at the entrance of the convent. The escape must therefore be made in the night from the 2nd to 3rd of June, but the cavalry officer had declared it utterly impossible if the captain, who was with him in the same room, was not won for the undertaking also. There was no stopping half way. I had to speak to the captain, and found him to be the most energetic man of the three. He accepted my propositions, and offered to take with him, as an escort, twenty-five men, which was very acceptable. In case that he should lose his life in the undertaking five thousand pesos were to be paid to his family immediately. That we should all be cut down if overtaken, he was certain.

The next day the Emperor wrote the following bill of exchange, which is still in my possession :—

QUERETARO, *June 1st*, 1867.

The bank house — —, in — — has to pay to the family of Captain — —, in case the latter should die, the sum of five thousand pesos (5000) *immediately.*

(Signed)   MAXIMILIAN.

The Emperor then told me to write down the following :—

" To procure a good guide to the Sierra Gorda ; to buy dark lanthorns ; to poison cavalry horses, or to make them unserviceable ; not to forget writing materials."

As the garrison left in Querétaro was not numerous, not many cavalry horses would have to be rendered unserviceable, or to be killed in order to make pursuit impossible.

When I came to see the Emperor, June 1st, about noon, and we spoke much about our escape, the question was treated, whether Dr. Basch was to be made acquainted with the project. The Emperor was against it; he said, "Dr. Basch is a faithful soul, but I am afraid that he would betray us by his nervous manner. As he, however, might become aware that something was preparing, we had better tell him that I was probably going to San Luis Potosi, and that you only would be permitted to go with me. To make that appear more likely let him give you some prescriptions for me which I shall require under any circumstances."

He remarked also that when he was in luck he had many persons about him who tried their best to please him, and said, "I regret, Salm, that you have only to share the bitter with me, but I hope to God better times will come."

As we discussed the difficulty caused by the situation of our cells in different stories, and the possibility of our separation, we agreed what we should do in that case, and also if only one of us should succeed. I said, "That I certainly would give myself up again if the Emperor should be retaken or prevented from escaping;" but he answered, "No, I do not want you to do that by any means; I order you positively to go." On my question where he wanted me to go in such a case, he directed me to go on board the Austrian ship, " Elizabeth," in the harbour of Vera Cruz, and gave me the following letter for her captain :—

QUERETARO, *June* 1, 1867.

DEAR CAPTAIN VON GROELLER,—I send you with the present my general and aide-de-camp, Prince Salm, now chief of my household, recommending him to you most warmly. Take him on board of your ship in order to wait there for me or my instructions.

Your affectionate
(Signed) MAXIMILIAN.

The departure of my wife to Mexico had been delayed, as no conveyance was to be had; and I was glad of it, as my confidant officer told me that everything was prepared for the escape. He and his two associates mounted guard at noon the 2nd June, to remain there for forty-eight hours. I saw the Emperor at one o'clock and it was definitively resolved to make our escape the same night.

Everything was as favourable as could be. The only person we had to fear was Colonel Palacios. For his ferocious appearance, which was still increased by his squinting, the Emperor, who liked to give people nicknames, called him the "hyena." He was, however, not quite so ferocious as he looked, and was out of the way, as he had his lodging in one of the two courts of the convent, which was very remote from ours. The guards commanded by our three officers were the only ones in the convent, and Mexican soldiers do not think, but merely do what they are ordered. In the city were but few soldiers, and small patrols went through the streets only until eleven o'clock p.m. As we were all armed, and had twenty-five horsemen with us, a chance rencontre was not dangerous. There were no posts outside the city, and no troops whatever between it and the Sierra Gorda.

When I walked in the passage smoking a cigar, Miramon made me a sign. Watching for an opportunity, I dropped my cigar when I came near him. He handed me politely his box with matches, and on opening it I discovered beneath the few matches a paper. I lighted my cigar and then returned the match box; but according to Mexican politeness he declined, and I put it in my pocket directly before the sentinel, who stood about a yard from us. When I had an opportunity I read the following note:

" Mis caballos han sido tomados ayes, de

Joh. Lindner, München sc.

Miguel Miramon

consiguiente no tengo, en cuanto à los pistolos estanacon migo. Quisiera saber la manera como N. tiene arreglado esto, por que temo mucho si no una *traicion*, si una maladireccion, que pueda costarmi la vida aminado (!), escribamelo N. al momento.—Vuestre amigo. " M. M."

On this day Miramon had the melancholy pleasure of seeing his wife, who had arrived from Mexico with his infant child, two months old.

At one o'clock p.m. a telegraphic despatch arrived, announcing that Baron Magnus and the two best lawyers of Mexico, Martinez de la Torre and Riva Palacio, the father of the general, had started for Querétaro.

The Emperor sent for me about five o'clock and told me that the journey of my wife was not necessary now, and *that he would not escape that night!*

If a thunderbolt had fallen at my feet, I could not have been more aghast, for such a favourable opportunity for escape would never occur again. I implored the Emperor almost on my knees not to postpone his escape, especially as his reason for it was of so little account. " What would the ministers, whom I invited here, say ! " he exclaimed, " if they arrived and did not find me ! " " They would be heartily

glad to see you anywhere else," I replied. But
the Emperor remained firm, and tried to appease
my fear for his life, by saying, " They will not
be in such a hurry, and a few days more or less
will be of no account." It was almost the same
answer he gave me on the evening of the 14th
May. He is, however, not the only prince who
has had to mourn over a " too late !"

When I communicated to the officers of the
guard the resolution of the Emperor, I had the
utmost trouble to appease them, for they were
not only afraid of losing the promised reward,
but also of discovery. Too many persons knew
about the plan, and if not carried out that
night, it would certainly be betrayed; at present
nothing was yet known, and success was as
good as certain.

I saw the Emperor again, but he insisted
on the postponement of the escape until the
arrival of Baron von Magnus, in whom he had
great confidence, " as the same had assisted him
in everything so energetically and faithfully,
whilst those representatives, of whom he might
have expected assistance with far better right,
had acted miserably and almost in a hostile
manner. Had they not taken so much trouble
to induce the foreign troops to leave the country, they might have remained and have done
very good service."

He regretted very much that the English minister, Mr. Scarlett, had left Mexico, for he knew that he would have supported the endeavours of Baron von Magnus.

On June 3rd I was with the princess in the room of the Emperor. Alone with me he usually called me by my Christian name, but always with the wrong one, Filip instead of Felix. I never permitted myself to correct him, but my wife did. I mention this circumstance as the Emperor used this Christian name in an official document, and I had some trouble in proving that I was the person really meant and no other man. The Emperor presented each of us with his photograph, and wrote his name underneath.

On the 4th of June the Emperor rose earlier than usual, as he expected the foreign ministers, who disappointed him, however, that day. To while away the time he arranged a domino party in the niche formed by the passage before his cell, and Mejia, Miramon, and myself took part in it. The Emperor was to-day in very good spirits, and explained the game to Mejia, which seemed to tire Miramon, who looked at me with a smile of resignation. About noon came at last the very much longed for permission from Escobedo, for my removal to the cell which had been occupied until then alone by Dr. Basch.

In the evening I sat very long at the bedside

of the Emperor who was then rather low-spirited and melancholy. He placed his hand in mine, and made me the confidant of his sorrows in reference to his person and family. I do not feel at liberty to publish what he confided to me, and will only say that he spoke with the utmost love of the Empress, his consort, Archduchess Sophia, his mother, and his brother Archduke Charles Lewis. He expressed himself with some bitterness about the family act of renunciation which he had been induced to sign on accepting the Imperial crown of Mexico.

On June 5th, early in the morning, I received a visit from the infantry officer, my confidant, who told me that he was afraid his superior officers had heard something about their plan. If so, however, he was most to blame. He and his comrades could not forbear showing the gold they received from me, making thus their poorer fellow-officers suspicious and jealous. General Escobar, who was in the cell next mine, had warned me already once to be cautious when giving money to Liberal officers, as he had heard the chink of coin in my cell.

I suppose that the officers, on seeing that they were suspected, and to prevent worse consequences, divulged the whole affair 'to' their superiors, representing it only as a means to get money, and to ascertain the intention of the prisoners.

I heard also Madame General Miramon accused of having attracted suspicion by her talk, though I do not know how much foundation was in it. However, I had not to wait long for the consequences.

When I returned to my cell, leaving the Emperor alone with his physician, a Liberal general—I believe his name was Paz—entered, and, addressing me in a brutal manner, said: "You have attempted to effect the escape of Maximiliano. If you repeat it you will be shot on the spot."

Since the Emperor had refused to avail himself of the means prepared by me for his escape, I cared but little for anything, and least about the consequences which the discovery might have with respect to myself, and, annoyed by the tone of the general, I replied in the same key: "And if I had done as you say, should I have done more than my duty? You, I suppose, would have done the same if you had a feeling of honour and love for your chief. It is not the first time that I ventured my life for my Emperor; and am ready to venture it again to save him."

"We know that," answered the general,

"and Escobedo has told me that you were the man to carry it out. We will, therefore, bring you to a place where this will be made impossible;" and, casting threatening looks at me, he left the cell.

"You can do nothing but shoot me," I called after him; "but to-day our turn—to-morrow yours : that's Mexican fashion."

When the general had delivered me of his presence, I was ashamed that I had permitted myself to be carried away by my vexation, and I went to visit the Emperor, to take an invigorating example from the serene dignity with which he bore his cross.

An officer soon came with the order to follow him. He had no objection to my taking leave of the Emperor. When I saw him I could not utter one single word. He gave me his hand, which I covered with kisses. I felt as if I might not look on his dear face again. At the door I again looked round. Two silent tears ran down the august martyr's cheeks. That was too much. My heart was breaking.. I rushed to my room, and gave vent to my grief by loud sobs.

I soon recovered, however, and placed myself at the disposal of the officer, indifferent even if he led me to the place of execution. He conducted me, however, downstairs to the cell of the other generals, whom, to my surprise, I found all ready to start. Afraid of further attempts at escape, Escobedo had given orders that all the prisoners, with the exception of the Emperor, Miramon, and Mejia, should be removed from the convent.

Surrounded by an extraordinary numerous escort, under the command of Colonel Palacios, we had to walk slowly through the streets, under a burning sun, to the casino, the place where all the field-officers were confined, whilst the subaltern officers had remained in the convent San Teresita. We were conducted into a large hall, where the Emperor held a drawing-room immediately after his arrival. A guard separated us from the rest of the prisoners. The above-mentioned general came and favoured us with a speech, in which he regretted that he was compelled to use more strictness than hitherto, by events that had occurred within the last few days; on saying which he looked significantly at me.

To his great displeasure, Dr. Basch had been obliged to make this forced march with us. He paced the large hall in mute fury, and at last laid down on a table to sleep it off. After a nap of an hour, he was, however, awakened and brought back to the Emperor.

The stricter measures announced by the general were soon manifest. The guards were trebled; our servants not permitted to enter; wine prohibited, and knives and forks taken away from us. The general was probably afraid that we should attack his valiant guard with our forks, and so escape !

I was much amused to see fourteen generals and as many colonels eat their meat with their fingers instead of knives; but these gentlemen would not see the humour of the thing, were angry with me, and requested me to forego all schemes for escape, which only served to make their position more disagreeable.

General Escobar, who became at a later period, with General Castillo, my best friend, expressed himself in the most severe terms. I became angry myself, and the consequence was a pistol duel, to be fought the first day after our release.

I forgot to mention that Baron von Magnus, accompanied by his chancellor, Mr. Edouard Scholler, the two advocates, and the Belgian Secretary of Legation Hooricks, had arrived about noon. I was very glad to see the baron a few moments with the Emperor. He had rendered me many services, and I had been much in his company. I felt very much reassured by his being near the Emperor, who now would miss me less.

The Emperor acknowledged my endeavours to serve him in a very flattering manner, by saying, in my presence, to Baron Magnus: "The prince fought like a lion, and proved the truest friend in misfortune." I ought not to mention it myself; but as this word of my Emperor is my dearest and only reward for my devotion to him, I will run the risk of being thought vain.

On the 6th of June at last also arrived the Austrian *chargé d'affaires*, Baron von Lago, with his secretary, Knight Schmidt de Tavera, and the Italian minister, Curtopassi.

To save troops, and not for the sake of humanity, the guard was removed to-day which separated us from the field-officers. I, therefore, had the pleasure of again seeing my friends, Lieut.-Colonels Pitner, Count Pachta, and Major Malburg, and also Major von Goerbitz. The last-named four gentlemen lived in the same room, and we celebrated our meeting with a bowl of brandy-punch, which we procured for money from soldiers' wives, and by a rubber of whist.

On the 7th of June a colonel of Escobedo's staff made another speech to us, warning us to forbear from all intrigues to escape,

and threatening us that we should be immediately shot on detection. These good people
were always afraid of us, and not without good
reason; for the good-will of most of the inhabitants of Querétaro was with us.

ON June 8th came from San Luis Potosi the order that the Emperor and all generals were to be placed before a court-martial, under the law of January 2nd, 1862. Such a court-martial and death were synonymous. The court was ordered to be appointed by the supreme government. The charges against the accused were examined by the assessor of the commanding general, and, if found correct, the judgment was to be executed by order of that general. There was no appeal against such a judgment nor was any grace allowed.

All the other officers were punished quite arbitrarily, without a trial. All colonels were condemned to six years' criminal imprisonment, the lieut.-colonels to five years, the majors to four, the captains and foreign lieutenants to two years. All Mexican lieutenants were set free, but had to return home, where they were to be placed under military surveillance for one year.

Besides this, General Escobedo was directed

to pick out from all grades those officers against whom there were particular charges, and to bring them also before a court-martial.

According to this order, I, as colonel, should have been condemned to six years' criminal imprisonment, and would have to commence it at once, as was ordered also. The idea of being still more separated from the Emperor, under the present circumstances, was intolerable to me, and to prevent it I presented my general's commission. The Liberal colonel of the staff was fair enough to draw my attention to the little circumstance that the law of January 2nd, 1862, meant death to every one captured in arms, and that no grace was to be expected. He offered to keep silence about my being a general, but I refused.

On the 9th of June the Austrian *chargé d'affaires*, Baron von Lago, came to see the imprisoned Austrian officers, Pitner, Pachta, and Malburg. With the baron came his secretary, as I suppose in honour of his very Mexican name of Schmidt, in Mexican costume.

Though Baron Lago knew me very well, as he had seen me frequently in the house of Baron Magnus, in Mexico, and the Emperor had informed him expressly of the relations between him and myself, the great diplomatist did not think it convenient to take the slightest notice of me, and his Sancho Panza, the Mexicanized Chevalier Schmidt, imitated him. Being much amused at this, I ran right against the baron, and thus compelled him to acknowledge my presence by a hurried salute.

The captains had been led outside the city already at noon, and were waiting for the field-officers. The latter assembled in the yard of the casino, and those only remained who had been picked out for the favour of a court-martial. These were the Colonels Monterdo, Reyes, Othon, Redonet, Diaz, and Rodriguez; the Lieut.-Colonels Pitner and Almanza; and a number of majors and subaltern officers. Amongst the former was Major von Goerbitz, who owed this distinction to Dr. Licea, whom he insulted as he deserved when that worthy betrayed Miramon.

Among those reserved for court-martial were, besides the Emperor, Miramon, and Mejia, the following generals: Castillo, Casanova, Herera y Lozado, Ramirez, Moret, Valdez, Escobar, Liceago, Calvo, Salm-Salm, and Magana. The latter was a man past eighty, who had not fought for twenty years, and whom none of us knew.

Of the civil officers reserved for court-martial were the Minister Garcia Aguirre, the Prefect

Dominiquez, the Commissary Tomas Prieto, and the Secretary of the Emperor, Luis Blasio.

The Fiscal of the Republican Government was Lieut.-Colonel Aspirez, a good-looking young man of twenty-eight, whom Juarez had picked out expressly for this purpose. The Assessor of Escobedo was Escoto, a young fellow of twenty, who had a very bad and ferocious expression in his features, but was an entirely submissive tool in the hands of Escobedo.

Fifty field-officers, who stood in the yard of the casino, were to be transported to Morelia; amongst them were Pradillo and Ormachea. It was very hard to me to part from these my faithful companions in arms, and the more so as all of us had a very dark future before us. The manner in which the Republican Government treated these field-officers was revolting, but was characteristic of the spirit of this government. These officers (amongst whom were many old men, and others who were disabled or weakened by their wounds) had to march on foot, in the heat of a Mexican summer, and each with his bundle on his back, for sixteen days to Morelia, escorted by a detachment of cavalry.

As these officers had been always on horseback, they were not used to a march on foot in the heat of the sun, and on sandy roads, and the consequence was that many of them suffered from sore feet and other marching complaints. After the second day they therefore declared that they could not walk any longer, but preferred to be shot.

The citizens of Celaya received these unfortunate men with great kindness. They offered them not only all kinds of victuals and refreshments, but even mules, and requested permission to sell them on their arrival, and to buy with the money some commodities for themselves. Similar to this was their reception in other places.

Fifty of the captains were sent to Guanajato, fifty to Zacatecas, and seventy-two to San Luis Potosi. Amongst the latter were also the foreign lieutenants. All these prisoners were not treated as prisoners of war, but to the disgrace of Escobedo, who broke his word, were placed on a level with robbers and thieves.

On the 9th of June, in the evening, my faithful shadow, Lieutenant Montecon, came to say farewell to me. The brave boy wept like a child. He told me that he would find means to enter Mexico, and fight again against the Liberals. Since that time I have never heard of him.

On the 10th of June the Princess succeeded in procuring permission for me to see the Emperor. Accompanied by Major Longoria, of Escobedo's staff, I went with her through the city. The Emperor was sick, but had preserved his serene, manly composure, though he owed it to himself and to others to do all that was possible to save his life. We examined all chances for it, but none remained but escape, and we by no means despaired of success, though all precautions had been taken to render it more difficult. Two field officers, armed with revolvers, continually guarded the door of the Emperor during night; that is, one of them slept in the before-mentioned niche, the other walked up and down the passage.

If an escape could be effected, we were to go next to the Sierra Gorda, from thence to the Rio Grande, and thence to Vera Cruz. In that city the Emperor expected to find more than a million of dollars in the treasury, and as the Mexicans had no fleet to prevent it, we could procure provisions from Havana, and troops from the State of Yucatan, which was in favour of the Emperor. Thus we might be enabled to hold out for at least a year, whilst Miramon and Mejia were busy in the country. A year is a very long time in Mexico, and the cause of the Emperor might again take a favourable turn.

For the execution of our projects, it was desirable that I should be again quartered near the Emperor. He requested Escobedo to permit this, but was refused; however, it was allowed that I should visit him, accompanied by an officer of the staff.

In the morning of the 11th of June, we were again transferred to the convent San Teresita, which offered more facilities for guarding us than the casino, and which had become empty by the departure of the subaltern officers. Here we were guarded by the battalion of Supremos Poderes, the lifeguard of President Juarez; therefore, as I suppose, an *elite* corps. Still they were a most miserable corps, and the most blackguardly, despicable rabble. This was less the fault of the soldiers than that of their commanders. The field-officers paraded in splendid sparkling uniforms, with kid gloves of the most delicate shades, and bedizened with heavy gold chains, whilst the subaltern officers begged from the prisoners, and were happy to accept a shilling !

The soldiers importuned us always, begging for a clacko ; and even the sentinels, who held in one hand their musket, stretched out the other for alms. When we dined they surrounded our table like hungry dogs, and I have actually seen one of them quarrel with a dog for a small piece of bread thrown to the latter.

As there were several of my old Cazadores amongst the Supremos Poderes, I heard from them many particulars. They received only twice a week pay for half a day, and their meals consisted of very thin coffee, with a good deal of sugar in the morning—for sugar costs very little; for dinner, beans with tortillas, and for supper the same. Of meat they got only an ounce or two now and then.

As the officers were afraid that the soldiers might run away, they were always locked up, and those who complained about it, or about the curtailment of their pay by their superiors, were flogged, and received up to three hundred lashes. For such a purpose, the battalion formed a hollow square, and the delinquent was laid down in the middle. The corporals, one after the other, applied the beating, whilst music played, or drums and fifes made a great noise to drown the cries.

On the 12th of June, I had permission to see the Emperor. Baron Magnus had gone to San Luis Potosi, to try his best again with Juarez, for orders had been sent by him to proceed with the court-martial against the Emperor, and the Generals Miramon and Mejia. It was to commence next morning in the Iturbide Theatre; though there were plenty of more proper places in Querétaro, the theatre was selected, I suppose, either to mortify the prisoners, if not to indicate that the whole law proceeding was only a cruel farce.

Desperate as the position of the Emperor was, he never lost his serene dignity. When I came, he gave me his hand and said, "Now Salm, everything will be over soon." He had just laid aside a book which he had been reading. I looked at the title, and saw that it was the "History of King Charles I. of England." When I told Miramon of it, he said, "It was reading fit for the situation." Before this, the Emperor had read the "History of Frederick the Great." He always read historical or scientific books, and had an aversion to novels.

Upon this occasion, I stayed a long time with the Emperor, and spoke with him about a great variety of different things.

As the Emperor knew that I was acquainted with several officers of Escobedo's staff, and even certain negociations were going on between some of them and myself, of which I shall speak immediately, he gave me some instructions which could only be fulfilled by their help. He made three requests, which I had to write down in my note-book :—1. That good marksmen might be selected for his execution; 2. That these should aim at his breast; and 3. That he should be shot at one and the same moment with his two generals, Miramon and Mejia.

Besides this, the Emperor dictated to me

the following distribution of decorations. Baron
Magnus, the commander's cross of the order of
the Eagle; his chancellor, Mr. Scholler, the
cross of the Guadelup order; Dr. Basch, the
officer's cross of the same; Captain Pawlowski,
and Lieutenant Koehlich, of the hussars, the
cross of the Guadelup order, and General Prince
Salm-Salm, the commander's cross of the order
of the Eagle. At the same time, he told me
that he intended to decorate the Italian minister Curtopassi, but he did not know yet which
order he would give him, and said he would tell
me on the 14th, when he expected to see me
again. The Emperor told me also that he had
written to his mother, the Archduchess Sophia,
and that I, on my going to Europe, should
take that letter with me, and deliver it in person. I do not know what has become of this
letter, but so much do I know, that it had
not been received by the archduchess so
recently as February, 1868.

Though the Emperor was fully prepared to
die, this did not exclude his hope that he might
escape, which was to be arranged chiefly by
the princess, who intended to endeavour to
bribe two Liberal colonels with 100,000 pesos
each, for which the Emperor would sign drafts
on his family.

The Emperor spoke a great deal about his

plans for the future, if there should be a future
for him. Next he would sail in his yacht to
Cadiz, and settle there some of his faithful followers, of whom he named especially, Miramon,
Mejia, Castillo, and the Minister Aguirre; then
he would visit Lacroma, and meet somewhere
the Empress and his mother; the winter he
would either pass in Naples, or in the east, or
in Brazil. I was to accompany him everywhere.
He looked forward with delight to the moment when he might breathe the air of freedom
again on board his ship, and awakened similar
longing in me. "Your Majesty," I called out,
" I request, in advance, your pardon, if I should
get a little tipsy on that blessed day," which
the Emperor promised laughingly.

The Emperor requested me frequently, and
repeated it on that same night, to write the
history of his short reign, that the world might
become acquainted with the truth, and "justice
be done to his memory." I was to do all in my
power to get possession of the required documents, and, if necessary, even with the revolver
in my hand. He expressed this desire, even in
a codicil to his last will, as Dr. Basch knows,
who signed the codicil as a witness.

When I said good-night to the Emperor,
I did not think that I had seen his noble,
revered face for the last time!

On returning to San Teresita I found the
princess, and we had to converse much about
our plans.   Nothing had been decided yet, and
she was greatly excited.   She left me, however,
full of confidence in the assistance of heaven
in so good a cause, and in her own courage.

The 13th of June was the day appointed
for the commencement of the court-martial.
The president was a lieutenant-colonel, Plato
Sanchez, and the judges were very young
captains, of whom some could not even read
or write.   This Sanchez was killed later by his
own men.

At six o'clock a.m., fifty men of the Cazadores de Galeano, and fifty of the Guardia de
Supremos Poderes, were already placed before
the Capuchin convent, the court was to be
opened at eight o'clock.   As the Emperor was
sick, and not willing to appear before such a
mock court, the Generals Miramon and Mejia
were placed alone in a closed carriage, and
surrounded by a numerous escort.   They drove
to the Iturbide Theatre, where this judicial farce
was to be enacted.

The theatre was decked out with colours
and republican emblems, and brightly lighted up
as at any other representation.   All officers
present in Querétaro had received orders to
appear, and tickets had been given out to

citizens.   The ladies of Querétaro did not avail themselves of this opportunity, and only the wives of Liberal officers did so.   The judges in full uniform, and their heads covered, and the other actors in the piece, sat on the stage.

The trial has been already told, not only in the papers, but also in books upon that subject, so that I need not enter into any details, and the less so as according to my opinion, the lawyers might have saved their learning.   It was utterly thrown away before such a court-martial, and all they said could not have the slightest influence on the judges.   I will not even speak of their low state of education, which made them unable to understand the fine definitions and arguments in the excellent speeches for the defence, but merely state that these speeches could not get rid of the fact, that the Emperor had been captured with arms in his hands, and, therefore, as according to the law of January 25th, 1862, which had to be applied, every one was to be punished by death who was so captured, the judges could not pronounce any other sentence but guilty.

A similar sentence would have to be pronounced against all officers and privates captured in Querétaro, if the government had judged it convenient to place them before a court-martial.   That the government made exceptions, proves that it was in its power to make them; and that it did not make such an exception in the Emperor's case, which recommended itself more to mercy than any other by a concurrence of circumstances, was a proof that the government, when ordering a court-martial upon the Emperor, had positively resolved on his death.

Long-lasting civil wars demoralize every people, even the best, and they are not calculated, indeed, to improve the moral feelings of a people like the Mexicans, who have been always considered one of the most miserable upon the face of the earth. It is, therefore, not to be wondered at; but, on the contrary, is very natural, that the most sacred promises should have but little or no value whatever with them, even if guaranteed by all the monarchs of Europe. The Emperor had still a very strong party in the country, and had, since the departure of the French, shown an energy, which made it a question of life and death for the Juarez government not to keep promises under which he might be released. Death made an end of all these fears, and the security attained by it for the Juarez government outweighed by far the fear of a possible revenge from the European kings. They knew, moreover, with tolerable certainty, that this danger was not very great, and that no power would declare war against Mexico, merely to revenge the death of Maximilian, especially with the warning of the mighty Emperor of France before their eyes, who had earned nothing but disgrace from such a war.

There were, also, a great many people in the army who demanded revenge on the Emperor, and whose votes the President, whose term of office had been long since at an end, required for his re-election. A third motive, which also urged the government to decide on death was, as I was told by persons nearly related to the government, not to suffer the rare opportunity of revenging the Republican principle on that of the Monarchy which the capture of a crowned head had given them.

Recapitulating the reasons of Juarez for desiring the death of the Emperor, we find them to be : Fear of a resumption of the struggle, in spite of all promises, and the desire to satisfy the thirst for revenge of the army and the ultra-Republicans. Whether a vindictive disposition and cruelty should be placed amongst the reasons cannot be ascertained; but one might be justified in presuming such motives, considering the murder of San Jacinto and other similar cruelties ordered by Juarez.

I do not intend to give an account of the

trial of the Emperor Maximilian ; but refer every one who is interested in this singular mockery of a law proceeding to the excellent pamphlet published by the two eminent Mexican lawyers who defended him.* They saw at once that, from a legal point of view, they were utterly powerless against the explicit law of January 25th, 1862, which orders the punishment of death against every foreigner or Mexican captured in arms against the Republic, or who should assist its enemies in any manner.

In their pamphlet, the advisers of the Emperor, therefore, say : " To have a chance of success, it was necessary to base the defence on considerations of convenience, of peace, and the future advancement of our country. It was necessary to break the power of unfavourable fate by dividing it ; to make an energetic defence before the court-martial, and, on the other hand, to point out to the government the difficulties into which our country might come, by placing before their eyes the dangers of severity, and the incalculable advantages of moderation in the

* I saw only the German translation by Conrad Pascher, Consul of Mecklenburg, in Mexico. The title of it is "Denkschrift uber den Process des Erzherzogs Ferdinand Maximilian von Oestreich von Mariano Riva Palacino and Licct Rafael Martinez de la Torre." Hamburg. Otto Meissner, 1868.

exertion of their respective powers of punishing and pardoning."

This was the only practical way to prove to the government that it was more profitable to spare the life of the Emperor than to take it. But it was difficult, or rather impossible, of which the counsel for the defence soon became aware; for the advantages were uncertain and distant, whilst the gratification of the vengeance of the people deadened more urgent fears, and brought with it most intelligible advantages in regard to the re-election of Juarez.

Whilst the defence thus tried to put all actions of the Emperor into their best light, the counsel for the Republic endeavoured, of course, to prove, not only that he failed against the above-mentioned law, but tried, also, to give all the actions of Maximilian the darkest colouring, in order to justify the government of Juarez before the less blood-thirsty Republicans at home and abroad.

A single narration of the circumstances under which Maximilian accepted the crown was his best defence. After having refused it several times, he accepted at last when he had been convinced that it was the wish of the Mexican people, and after his conscience had been satisfied by the approbation of learned English lawyers, whom he might suppose to be impartial.

He believed in the honesty and truth of the election; for people in Germany are not very experienced in election stratagems, and he had not even an idea that similar artifices had been employed in Mexico as those which made Napoleon III. Emperor of France.

In this belief that he was the elect of the people, he could only be confirmed by his brilliant and enthusiastic reception in Mexico, his new country, the happiness of which he really wished to promote with all his heart.

The notion of treating him as a filibuster, which was only brought forward to prove him punishable with death, under another title, is not worth speaking of. The same may be said with regard to his having been a tool of the French. This was not so much the case as is supposed, for he cancelled the treaty which had been made by one of his ministers with the French ministry, relating to the cession of the State, Sonora, and removed the minister from his place. I will only dwell upon that one accusation which tells most against him, and for which he is much blamed, even by well-meaning people. I mean the law of October 3rd, 1865, which was issued by advice of Marshal Bazaine in opposition to that of Juarez of January 25th, 1862, and which it even surpassed in cruelty.

The draft of this law was made by Marshal

Bazaine himself, as I was told by the Emperor. It was represented to him as absolutely necessary to restore order, and especially against the numerous bands of brigands, who, under pretext of serving the Liberal government, devastated the villages, plundered the country, and made the highways dangerous. It could not be meant against a Liberal army, as such an army was then a fiction, as was even a Liberal government. Juarez had fled to Paso del Norte, close to the frontier of the United States, and it was even said, and believed, in Mexico, that he had left the territory of that empire. The draft was not severe enough for Marshal Bazaine, and he made some additions with his own hand.

The Emperor signed this law under the condition that it should be applied only against marauders and brigands, and even then only under his confirmation for each case. Nay, he even gave orders that, on the arrival of such a notice, upon which depended life or death, he should be awakened, even in the middle of the night, or disturbed in whatever important occupatiou he might be engaged. The fact is, that under the Emperor's confirmation, only a few robbers were executed, who had been already pardoned several times; and that the law— which is about the same as that of Juarez of January 25th, 1862—was discussed in the council of his Cabinet, and signed by all the ministers.

How Marshal Bazaine carried out the intentions of the Emperor is another question, and it is very probable that he made use of the law, which suited his purpose and taste, whenever he pleased, and without asking the Emperor. It would, however, be unjust to make the latter responsible for the transgressions of Bazaine or the French, for he had no means whatever of punishing them. Bazaine, differing in his opinion from that of the Emperor on some point, wrote him an impertinent letter, and it required the most earnest exertions of the Emperor, through the mediation of the French minister, to induce the marshal to apologize. The complaints transmitted to Paris were in vain; the French Emperor would not listen to them; for it is impossible to believe that he could not influence the marshal. The French insulted the Mexicans of their own party, and treated those of the opposite party with revolting cruelty. They stole everything they could lay their hands on; and, of the two loans, only nineteen millions found their way into the treasury of the State, while the war, according to the calculation of the French, cost above sixty millions.

The Emperor Maximilian had to bear the

whole odium of this French misrule; but the
Emperor of France had no scruples in breaking
the treaties which had been made, as he was
dissatisfied with Maximilian, who took the
alleged philanthropic plans of Napoleon as
seriously meant, and tried to carry them out in
perfect faith for the benefit of the Mexicans.
Napoleon was furious on finding that Maximilian would not support him in his robbery,
by preventing the cession of Sonora, which the
French thought already theirs;—in a word,
that he did not enter into his views in reference
to Mexico, which he considered only as an easy
prey, as a means to recruit the French finances,
and which he intended to leave to its fate after
he had gorged himself sufficiently with gold. If
not, why did he not support the Confederate
States? The sword of France thrown into
the balance might have altered the result
very much; and that Napoleon III. did not
see the necessity of assisting the Confederate
States for a lasting success in Mexico, nobody
will believe, not even if he said so himself.
What did he care what became of the Emperor Maximilian? For a Napoleon, countries,
nations, and people are only like men on a chess-
board; and whatever is respected in life, is to
him only a cipher in a calculation. In the high
policy which a Napoleon considers to be his

own province, his own person is his chief purpose and end; and next to him, France, because
he needs her as his handmaid.

The fortunate adventurer, Napoleon, had,
for his own purposes, however, placed a poor
Austrian archduke—whose rich mind longed
for a proper field of action—on a road where
he might make his fortune, and satisfy his philanthropic fancies to his heart's content, with a
people who offered a wider field for improve-
ment than any other. Should the plan not
succeed, Napoleon supposed he might always
get out at least without damage; and as to
what became of an archduke with liberal ideas,
that was very indifferent to him.

When the plan, in consequence of the
energetic notes of the United States, took an
unexpected turn, the French imagined they had
done enough to offer him the voyage home
under their protection; and they were quite
furious that he crossed this arrangement by his
resolution to remain in Mexico, only because he
did not think it reconcileable with his honour
to steal away from his place like a thief.
Honour! Of course that is a childish idea, to
be dismissed with a shrug of the shoulders.

By this refusal of Maximilian to commit a
disreputable action, Napoleon considered himself released from all his obligations and trea-

ties. The Emperor of Mexico was sacrificed, not so much for his own faults as for the atrocities committed by the French under the authority of their Emperor, and by which they stirred up to its utmost the hatred of the wild and bloodthirsty Mexicans. It is true Juarez was the axe that killed Maximilian, but the moral guilt falls upon Napoleon.

On the 13th of June, early in the morning, the princess came to see me about the escape of the Emperor, which was to take place next night. The Emperor had written the two drafts for one hundred thousand pesos each; Baron von Lago had also signed them at his request, and taken them with him to have them signed by the other ministers. The princess waited, of course, impatiently for them, as she had to arrange the affair with the two colonels in the afternoon. The signatures of the ministers were demanded by the two colonels as an additional security. One of the colonels was especially careful, and said that he entered into this business solely out of love for his only child, for whom he wished secure a fortune.

The Emperor had given to my wife his signet ring, and it was agreed that it should be returned to him by that person whom he might follow in confidence.

I wrote now a long letter to the Emperor, in which I explained the plan of his escape, and gave it to the princess, as she probably would not have time and opportunity for a longer conversation. This letter was given by the Emperor to Baron Lago, as he said, to prove, after his death, "to his family and others what had been the relations between us, and what I had risked for him." It was obviously the intention of the Emperor, in doing so, to prepare for me a friendly reception in Vienna and Brussels, on my return to Europe; but that letter has never been produced by Baron Lago, and the Belgian *chargé d'affaires*, M. Hooricks, told me only a few weeks ago, when I saw him in Munich, that Baron Lago had destroyed that letter on the next day, being afraid that it might cost me my life; as if the pockets of the ministers were likely to be examined! But Baron Lago is a very careful man, especially if lives are endangered, of which he gave another proof on the same day.

The Emperor sent Dr. Basch to the worthy representative of Austria for the two drafts signed by the ministers. When the doctor entered the room and told his errand, Baron von Lago, *charge d'affaires* of his Imperial and Royal Majesty of Austria, etc., in Mexico, ran distractedly about his room, tearing his hair and crying out piteously, "We cannot sign them! If we do, we shall all be hanged!"

The other ministers were less excited. They requested the doctor to represent to the Emperor that the two colonels, if really willing to save him, would certainly be satisfied with his signature alone.

Baron Lago, who had already signed in presence of the Emperor, cut off his signature, and the doctor returned to his master with the mutilated bills and the answers of the ministers, describing, of course, the despair of Baron Lago, and his fear of being hanged.

"What would it matter," said the Emperor Maximilian, "if he were hanged! The world would not lose much in him."

On the 14th of June I waited all the morning, with great anxiety, for news of the Princess, and this anxiety increased when noon arrived without my having heard anything of her. At last an Indian woman brought me an open note from her, telling me "that she must set off immediately for San Luis Potosi; that she was much grieved at not being able to see me, but that she was not at liberty to give me any explanation."

Still cudgeling my brain about the meaning of this mysterious note, I received a visit which gave me the key to the riddle. It was an officer on duty who requested me to follow him. He led me past the guard, and on his beckoning, we were followed by a corporal and three men. I was led into a small chapel situated in the same story, and the officer said, " I have orders to separate you from the rest of the prisoners. You have already once laid plans for the escape of Maximiliano, and will recollect what was said to you then. You have now tried again, although in vain, to bribe officers and soldiers, and will have to suffer .the consequences." On leaving, he instructed the sentinel at my door that " nobody should be permitted to speak or to communicate with the prisoner; he must neither write nor receive letters, and the cabo-quarto (corporal of the guard) will bring him his meals."

The reason of the journey of my wife was pretty clear now. The plan for escape had again failed, but I was not to be informed why on that day? The chapel in which I was placed adjoined a hall, in which were other of our prisoners. Of the folding doors separating the two rooms formerly, the opening only existed, and near it stood the sentinel. Opposite the door was the altar, and to its right, in a corner, on the stone floor, was my bed, that is, a blanket. In the wall, to the right of the entrance, was a window opening, not grated, looking on a small yard, which was surrounded by a wall fifteen feet high, which communicated by means of a door, with an open passage running around the larger convent yard. Near that door, which was mostly ajar, was another sentinel at the top of a staircase. The chapel was ornamented with horrible frescoes representing some most bloody scenes of martyrdom.

On the morning of the 15th of June I received a visit from one of the two colonels with whom I was best acquainted. My first question was how it fared with the Emperor. He said, "He is lost beyond all hope." About the miscarriage in the escape I heard from him the following account :—

"Neither he nor his friend would accept the drafts signed only by the Emperor, as the refusal of the ministers to sign them proved clearly that their payment was very doubtful. Both the colonels had families, and if they succeeded in saving the Emperor they would have to fly from their country, and to live abroad. Under these circumstances they must have an unquestionable security for their being able to live comfortably with their families in foreign parts, before engaging in such a dangerous undertaking."

The other colonel, who had only been tempted by the hope of securing a fortune for his child, recovered his republican virtue in face of a doubtful bill, and though he had given his word of honour not to divulge the project to any one, he informed Escobedo, although without betraying his comrade.

It may perhaps appear strange that Escobedo did not treat me more severely after the discovery of the first endeavour to escape, and that he did not even fulfil his sinister promises when my attempt to save the Emperor was repeated, which would certainly have been done in more civilized countries. But in these civil wars it frequently happened that generals became prisoners of other generals, who soon perhaps became again their prisoners. Attempts to escape occurred very frequently, and were considered as very excusable and natural, and were not punished with too much severity, in order not to create a precedent which might perhaps tell against themselves. Escobedo himself had once been a prisoner of Mejia, and condemned to be shot by a court-martial; but Mejia had not only assisted him in his escape, but even furnished him with money for it. What Escobedo expected his own friends to do for him, he could not punish too severely in friends of the Emperor, and he was satisfied with making such attempts impossible.

When Dr. Basch came yesterday morning

from the princess, whom he had seen on the part of the Emperor, he was arrested as he was leaving his house. Soon afterwards an officer entered the room of the princess, who had no suspicion yet, and politely requested her to follow him to General Escobedo. The Liberal chief said to her, in a sarcastic tone, "Madam, the air of Querétaro is very unhealthy; typhus is prevailing here. There is here also a very dangerous atmosphere, and if I were as free to go as you are, and not prevented by my duty, I would go away. For you it will be better by all means, and I desire much that you leave within two hours."

The princess answered, "I understand you perfectly, general, and see that you know all. If it is a crime that I tried to save my Emperor and the benefactor of my husband, you may punish me."

The general left the room without saying a word, and the princess returned home.

A short time afterwards an officer, with his cap on his head and armed with his sword, entered without knocking, and said, "Madam, you must travel in ten minutes. The carriage is at the door; make yourself ready." It was so, and near the carriage was a cavalry escort; my wife was a prisoner. She requested the officer to permit her to see me only for a moment, as it might be perhaps for the last time in life, but the officer replied, "That this was the very thing he was not permitted to do." At last, on the intercession of the colonel, who was present, and who told me all this as an eye-witness, the officer permitted her to send me the little note which I received by the Indian woman.

The "ten minutes" had passed long ago, when the princess stepped with her chamber-maid into the carriage, but when she heard the officer in command give the order, "To head-quarters!" she jumped out again, and declared positively that she would not see Escobedo. The officer insisted on carrying out his order, but my wife insisted on her refusal.

"Madam, I am on duty; I must bring you to headquarters."

"Bring me to prison, or wherever you like, but I do not go to General Escobedo."

"Madam!" replied the embarrassed officer, "I repeat I am on duty. You will force me to take measures of compulsion to bring you there."

"In no other way will you be able to take me to Escobedo!"

As the scene approached a catastrophe, which could not fail to arise in consequence of the conflict between feminine perseverance and military duty, the highly amused colonel again interceded, and requested the officer to wait until he had spoken to the general, whom he accordingly went to see.

The general laughed, and said that he would rather stand opposite a whole Imperial battalion than meet the angry Princess Salm, and ordered her to be brought at once to the place arranged.

Accompanied by an escort of cavalry, she drove to Santa Rosa, a village at the foot of the Sierra Gorda, where she was set at liberty, but warned not to return to Querétaro, under the threat of being imprisoned. In this village she wrote a letter, which the colonel transmitted to me, and went to San Luis Potosi, where she alighted in the house of Consul Bahnsen, who received her with great kindness.

At the same time as the princess was removed from Querétaro, the foreign ministers received also orders to leave within two hours. They were the Austrian, Belgian, and Italian *chargé d'affaires*; the French minister, Mr. Dana, who had, like Bazaine, married a Liberal lady, had not come himself, and Baron Magnus had not yet returned from San Luis.

The Austrian *chargé d'affaires* was so much afraid that he set off in the greatest hurry, taking with him the unsigned codicil to the last will of the Emperor. As the deed was, however, signed by three witnesses, Baron

Lago, Mr. Hooricks, and Dr. Basch, the Emperor declared that it must be valid.

As the diplomatists had their permission to confer with the Emperor from a higher authority, the minister, Don Sebastian Lerdo de Tejada, they might have refused the order of Escobedo to quit, and thus have deprived this peremptory order of its humiliating character, which was somewhat mortifying to the great powers whom they represented.

Baron Magnus, who was not so fearful, returned from San Luis and went to see the Emperor as usual without being prevented by Escobedo. Had the baron been in Querétaro, the whole thing would not have happened, for although he, as the Prussian minister, was not under the same obligations as the representatives of Austria and Belgium, he would have signed the bills, and if not honoured in Vienna, Prussia would have paid the trifle and saved the brother of the Emperor of Austria.

On the 16th of June I was strictly guarded in my chapel; but fellow prisoners who entered the little yard now and then, succeeded in whispering to me some snatches of news. In this manner I heard that the Emperor had been condemned to be shot. Three of the judges were for banishment, three for death, but the vote of the president decided.

About ten o'clock a.m., the colonel, who, in consequence of his position, had free access, came and told me that the verdict had been already confirmed by Escobedo, and that the Emperor, Miramon, and Mejia, would be shot between two and three o'clock.

I had procured pen and ink from the caboquarto and entreated the Emperor to let me accompany him on his last walk, which request would not be denied by Escobedo. The colonel undertook to carry my letter to the Emperor. But he returned at one o'clock and brought me the following message from my unfortunate sovereign, "He sent me his last embrace and thanked me for all I had done for him. He knew my devotion, and much as he should like to have me with him, he was afraid that I might be carried away by my passion, and commit myself in a manner which might cost me my life. He had made up his account with the world, and it would affect him too much to take leave of a person who was so dear to him."

I asked the colonel whether there was no hope left; but he answered, "None whatever; at three o'clock everything will be over." The colonel was very sad, for he would have saved the Emperor if it had depended on him alone. "Oh, I wish I had never become acquainted with Maximiliano!" he said; "I was his bitter enemy, but he has won me altogether by his serene, sublime demeanour, and his amiability. When I saw him just now, my heart was breaking, and I am not ashamed to say that I went aside and wept."

After the colonel had left me, I gave way to my grief. I threw myself down on my couch and hid my face before the intolerably stupid gaze of the sentinel. Presently I was startled by the sound of drums and military music. I jumped up with a beating heart to the window. Though the high wall barred the view, I could distinctly hear the command of the officers placing their troops in the Alameda, which was only about three hundred paces distant; and as Mendez had been shot there, I imagined that the Emperor would be shot here also.

It was past two o'clock. I listened in breathless agony, for as I heard every word of command, I could not fail to hear also the fatal shots. But instead of them I heard merry music, and at three o'clock everything was silent.

My excitement was now indescribable, and can only be understood by one who has been in a similar situation. Hopes of the wildest character and the most hopeless despair chased each other in my soul; it was a horrible agony which I could not feel even if I was myself to be led to death. This silence became most oppressive from minute to minute, and thus passed two horrible hours.

At last, at about five o'clock, the colonel rushed into my chapel and said, " By order of the President, the execution has been postponed until the 19th inst. !" I could not forbear to embrace the friendly enemy and asked, " Do you think him saved ?" " I will not awaken false hopes in you, but according to my opinion he is saved." I heard from the colonel what had occurred. The day before news had already arrived that the Empress had died. Miramon and Mejia were in doubt whether this news should be communicated to the Emperor, but at last Mejia decided that it would be better, and he undertook to impart this sad news to his sovereign. It was well he did, for though the first impression was very painful, this news made death easier to him. The thought of his Empress tormented him more than anything else. He soon recovered from the first emotion, and said, to Dr. Basch, " One string less that binds me to life."

EXECUTION OF THE EMPEROR.

IN the morning of the 16th of June, at eleven o'clock, Colonel Miguel Palacios came, accompanied by General Refugio Gonzales, with a detachment of soldiers, and the latter read the death warrant to the Emperor and the two generals. The Emperor heard it with a calm smile, and looking at his watch, he said to Dr. Basch, "Three o'clock is the hour; we have still more than three hours, and can easily finish all."

The fatal hour came, and the three condemned waited in the passage for the officer charged with their execution. They waited a whole hour, and the Emperor conversed as usual with his confessor and two of his counsellors. At last came, at four o'clock, Colonel Palacios with a telegram from San Luis Potosi, ordering the postponement of the execution until June 19th. This news produced a most disagreeable impression on the Emperor, for he had done with life, and looked on this delay rather as a cruelty, knowing the Mexicans too well to believe in

Queretaro — 13. de Junio d

Las dos libranzas á
que firmé hoy para
Palacios y Villanueva
pagadas por la casa
de Austria — en Viena
que el dia de mi con
cedida á los subvencio

Max.

1867.

mil pesos

coroneles

se deben dar

milicia Imperial

no son validas

la salvacion

os coroneles

l'amor

grace. The troops who had been placed near the Alameda, to be marched from there to the Cerro de la Campaña, where the execution was to take place, were discontented also, fearing that they might be perhaps deprived of their victim. They had arrived with merry music, but returned home silent and sullen.

When the colonel left me, I abandoned myself to unrestrained joy. I ordered a bottle of wine to drink good luck to the Emperor, and smoking my cigar and humming a tune I paced my chapel, and even the horrid faces of the martyrs on the wall seemed to smile. The sentinel stared at me with his mouth wide open, probably thinking me mad. To give him a better idea of my wits, I presented him with four reals, but as he could not see any more reason for my present than for my good humour, I am afraid I only confirmed his bad opinion of the state of my brain.

On the 17th of June I awoke in very good spirits. I had slept excellently on my hard couch, and across my dreams I heard continually the joyful news, " The Emperor is saved!" This sorrow removed from my heart, I began to think of my own position. I was a prisoner, and wanted to be free. When I was sitting, yesterday, near my window, I heard the rolling of a carriage quite close to me, and I therefore concluded that the little yard was separated from the street only by one wall. This wall was about fifteen feet high from the yard; but as the yard was one story high, the wall rose from the street about thirty-five feet. To become free, I had to climb that wall. Through the ungrated window I might easily get into the yard; but how to get on the top of the wall, and down into the street, I did not yet know.

Whilst reflecting about it, I noticed some very heavy hooks in the gilt carved wood-work near the altar, which served, probably, to hold draperies. These would serve my purpose. If I had two or three of them, I might insert them between the stones into the wall, and climb it by this means. But how to get these hooks? Of course, the sentinel must help me to them.

"Amigo," I said, "I will give you two reals if you will take out these hooks, which I require for hanging up my clothes."

The Republican was all over smiles. He placed his musket in a corner, and commenced his work with a good will.

He could, however, only get out three hooks; the fourth stuck as deep as an old prejudice, and I had to be satisfied. I took my three hooks, and the Indian his gun and my two reals, with which he stealthily coquetted now and then, promenading, in hungry imagination, amongst mountains formed by tortillos, and longing for the relief. In order not to create suspicion, I fixed my hooks slightly in the wall, and had trouble to fill them all with my scanty wardrobe.

But how to find a rope, which I required to let down from the wall into the street? I thought of my wife. She might have procured me one, but she was in San Luis; and Escobedo had threatened to put her in prison if she returned. I could not forbear laughing when I thought that Escobedo imagined he could prevent her by that means. As I well knew, his threats were the best means to bring her back soon. I might wait until her arrival. She had promised me a mattress, and in it might be a rope with knots. Even the sentinels might help me to climb the wall. I was sure they would do it, for no Indian, with or without a gun, could resist the persuasive smile of one or two golden ounzes. In the street were, of course, horses ready, and away we went to join the Emperor! I went up and down my chapel, caressing with my eye the hooks, which appeared to me a very important acquisition. The chapel, the whole world, appeared to me, to-day, *couleur de rose*.

Colonel Villanueva had promised to come at

one'clock; but I waited in vain for him all day, and my doubts returned. What has happened? Should the bloody Indian, Juarez, or his Mephistopheles, Lerdo, the minister with the false, sarcastic mouth, dare still to commit the refined cruelty of murdering my Emperor, after having made him pass through all the bitterness of death? Maybe he offended their low souls by the nobleness of his demeanour. It would be an infamous cruelty; but what might not be expected from Mexicans!

On the morning of the 18th of June, Lieut.-Colonel Pitner came for a moment into the little yard, and whispered that things went very badly for the Emperor; and soon afterwards Colonel Villanueva came. He was greatly excited, and told me that he had been cruelly disappointed; Maximilian was lost without any hope; the execution would take place at eight o'clock next morning. "I am ashamed," he said, "that so many bad elements are amongst us. I hoped still that the Moderate party would conquer, and the life of the Emperor be saved. I feel grieved that my poor country, hated and despised by all the world, must be stained again in this manner!"

The Emperor had, on the 17th, already taken leave of his officers in Querétaro in the following letter :—

QUERETARO, PRISON DE LOS CAPUCINOS, *June* 17, 1867.

*To the Generals and Field-Officers, prisoners
in this city.*

At this solemn moment I address to you
the present lines, in order both to acknowledge
the loyalty with which you have served me,
and to give you a token of the true regard
which I feel for you.

Your affectionate   MAXIMILIAN.

As I was separated from the rest of the
prisoners, I saw this letter only later, and
therefore my name, as that of some other generals, is wanting under the reply.

Baron Magnus returned on the 18th from
San Luis Potosi, and visited the Emperor about
noon. He repeated his visit in the evening,
and stayed a long time with the Emperor, who
also remembered me in his conversation, and
said that he would never have suffered me to
leave him, had he been spared.

The Emperor ordered Dr. Basch to make a
list of persons to whom he desired to leave
some little keepsake. To me he bequeathed
his beloved perspective-glass, which he held
almost constantly in his hand during the entire
siege of Querétaro, and to the Princess the fan
which he had used in prison during his last
days. The Emperor went to bed at half-past

eight, and was already asleep when he was disturbed by a visit from Escobedo, at eleven o'clock p.m.

Captain Enking, who accompanied the general at this improper visit, will have noticed that the Emperor looked with an expression of intense expectation on the entrance of the general, as if expecting to hear news of his pardon from him. Had the captain observed correctly, the look of the Emperor would have been very explicable and natural. He could not, indeed, expect from Escobedo a visit of friendly sympathy, or believe that he only came to enjoy the ⌊sight of his foe conquered solely by vile treason. A visit from the commander-in-chief, under these circumstances, was solely justifiable if, disturbing the last sleep of his prisoner, he came to announce life to him.

From the Emperor, Escobedo went to see Mejia, who saved him once when he was condemned to be shot! Mejia recommended his children to him, and Escobedo promised to take care of them. He sent later an aide-de-camp to the general's widow, and offered her his assistance for her children, but the noble woman spurned the assistance of the murderer of her husband with scorn, and said that she was young and strong, and could work for her children.

I do not know for certain, whether Escobedo also saw Miramon. This general reproached himself very much in his last days. He said to Mejia he regretted that the bullet which pierced his cheek had not passed through his head, for it was chiefly owing to him that the Emperor found himself in his present position. Mejia told this to the Emperor and the latter told it to me.

In the afternoon of the 18th the Emperor telegraphed to Juarez. "I would desire that M. Miguel Miramon, and Thomas Mejia, who suffered all the tortures and bitterness of death, the day before last, might be spared, and that I, as I have already said, when taken prisoner, may be the only victim."

This request was refused, and the same fate attended the request of the same date of Baron Magnus, addressed to the minister Lerdo de Tejada, which thus concluded :—

. "I implore you, in the name of humanity and of Heaven, not to make any further attempt against his life, and repeat how certain I am that my sovereign his Majesty the King of Prussia, and all the monarchs of Europe, who are related to the imprisoned prince, his brother the Emperor of Austria, his cousin the Queen of Great Britain, his brother-in-law the King of Belgium, and his cousin the Queen of Spain, as also the Kings of Italy and Sweden, will readily agree to give all possible guarantee, that none of the prisoners shall ever return to Mexican territory."

The Emperor addressed letters of thanks to his four advisers, and wrote the following letter to Juarez, which is dated the 19th of June, as it was to be delivered on that day.

QUERETARO, *June* 19, 1867.

M. BENITO JUAREZ,—On the point of suffering death, because I desired to try whether new institutions would enable me to put an end to the bloody war which for so many years has been causing ruin to this unhappy country, I will yield up my life with satisfaction, if this sacrifice can contribute to the welfare of my adopted country.

" Being fully convinced that nothing durable can be produced on a soil soaked in blood and moved by violent agitations, I implore you in the most solemn manner, and with that sincerity which is peculiar to moments like those in which I find myself, that my blood may be the last that may be spilled, and that the same perseverance, which I appreciated when in the midst of prosperity, and with which you defended the cause that conquers now, might be applied to the most noble end; to reconcile all the hearts, and to rebuild on a durable, firm foundation, the peace and the order of this unhappy country.

(Signed) MAXIMILIAN.

In the morning of the 19th, at four o'clock, all were up in our convent, for the disposable part of the battalion Supremos Poderes marched out at half-past four. Soon after six o'clock, Lieut.-Colonel Pitner came into the room adjoining the chapel, and called out, " They have already led him away.'"

We now listened with breathless anxiety; but nothing betrayed what had happened, when on a sudden all the bells of the city began ringing after seven o'clock. Pitner called out, " He is dead now!" and not caring for the sentinel at my door, he rushed into the chapel, and in a mute embrace our tears fell in memory of the much beloved, noble dead. Towards eight o'clock the troops returned from the execution.

The last moments of the Emperor have been frequently described; but all these descriptions differ from each other. Though it was not my lot to assist my Emperor in his last moments, I shall write down what eight or ten Liberal officers, amongst whom was Colonel Villanueva, concurred in stating.

The Emperor rose as early as half-past

three, and made a very careful toilet. He wore a short dark (blue or black) coat, black pantaloons and waistcoat, and a small felt hat. At four o'clock Pater Soria came, from whom the Emperor had already received the last sacraments. At five o'clock a mass was celebrated, for which purpose an altar had been placed in the frequently mentioned niche.

The Emperor gave to Dr. Basch several commissions and greetings to his friends, amongst whom he did not forget to mention me. He then breakfasted at a quarter to six. The people in the city were much excited, and this excitement was even noticeable amongst some portion of the troops. Escobedo was afraid of demonstrations, and even of a riot, and in order to baffle such attempts, the execution was ordered to take place an hour sooner.

With the stroke of six o'clock the Liberal officer came to take the Emperor. Before he had yet spoken the Emperor said, "I am ready;" and came from his cell, where he was surrounded by his few servants, who wept and kissed his hands. He said, " Be calm ; you see I am so. It is the will of God that I should die, and we cannot act against that."

The Emperor then went towards the cells of his two generals, and said, " Are you ready, gentlemen ? I am ready." Miramon and Mejia came forward, and he embraced his companions in death. Mejia, the brave, daring man, who hundreds of times had looked smilingly into the face of grim death, was weakened by sickness, and very low-spirited.

All three went down the staircase, the Emperor in advance with a firm step. On arriving at the street before the convent he looked around, and drawing a deep breath, he said, "Ah, what a splendid day! I always wished to die on such a day."

He then stepped with Pater Soria into the next carriage waiting for him, the *fiacre* No. 10; for the Republican Government thought it probably below its dignity to provide a proper carriage for a fallen Emperor. Miramon entered the *fiacre* No. 16, and Mejia No. 13, and the mournful procession commenced moving. At its head marched the Supremos Poderes. The carriages were surrounded by the Cazadores de Galeano, and the rear was brought up by the battalion Nueva Leon, which was ordered for the execution.

Though the hour had been anticipated, the streets were crowded. Everybody greeted the Emperor respectfully, and the women cried aloud. The Emperor responded to the greetings with his heart-winning smile, and perhaps compared his present march with his entrance

and reception into Querétaro four months ago.
What a contrast! However, the people kept
quiet, and could not muster courage for any
demonstration; only from the azoteas the soldiers were favoured with odious names and
missiles.

On arriving at the Cerro de la Campaña the
door of the Emperor's *fiacre* could not be opened.
Without waiting for further attempts to do so,
the Emperor jumped to the ground. At his side
stood his Hungarian servant Tudos. On looking around he asked the servant, "Is nobody
else here?" In his fortunate days everybody
strove to be near him, but now on the way to
his untimely grave only a single person was
at his side! However, Baron Magnus and
Consul Bahnsen were present, though he could
not see them.

Pater Soria dismounted as well as he could.
The comforter required, however, comfort from
the condemned. He felt sick and fainting,
and with a compassionate look the Emperor
drew from his pocket a smelling-bottle which
my wife had given him, and which is said to be
now in the possession of the widowed Empress
of Brazil, and held it under his nose.*

The Emperor, followed by Miramon and

* I was told this by the lady of Minister Aguirre, who heard
it from his friend Pater Soria.

Mejia, who had to be supported, now moved towards the square of soldiers, which was open towards the Cerro. The troops for the execution were commanded by General Don Jesus Diaz de Leon. Where the square was open, a kind of wall of adobes had been erected. In the middle, where the Emperor was to stand, who was taller than his two companions, the wall was somewhat higher. On the point of taking their respective positions, the Emperor said to Miramon, " A brave soldier must be honoured by his monarch even in his last hour, therefore permit me to give you the place of honour," and Miramon had to place himself in the middle.

An officer and seven men now stepped forward, until within a few yards before each of the three condemned. The Emperor went up to those before him, gave each soldier his hand and a Maximilian d'or (twenty pesos), and said, " Muchachos (boys), aim well, aim right here," pointing with his hand to his heart. Then he returned to his stand, took off his hat, and wiped his forehead with his handkerchief. This and his hat he gave to Tudos, with the order to take them to his mother, the Archduchess Sophia. Then he spoke with a clear and firm voice the following words :—

" Mexicans ! persons of my rank and origin are destined by God either to be benefactors of the people or martyrs. Called by a great part of you, I came for the good of the country. Ambition did not bring me here; I came animated with the best wishes for the future of my adopted country, and for that of my soldiers, whom I thank, before my death, for the sacrifices they made for me. Mexicans! may my blood be the last which shall be spilt for the welfare of the country; and if it should be necessary that its sons should still shed theirs, may it flow for its good, but never by treason. Viva independence! viva Mexico!"

Looking around, the Emperor noticed, not far from him, a group of men and women who sobbed aloud. He looked at them with a mild and friendly smile, then he laid both his hands on his breast, and looked forward. Five shots were fired, and the Emperor fell on his right side, whispering slowly the word "Hombre." All the bullets had pierced his body, and each of them was deadly; but the Emperor still moved slightly. The officer laid him on his back, and pointed with the point of his sword on the Emperor's heart. A soldier then stepped forward, and sent another bullet into the spot indicated.

Neither the Emperor, nor Miramon, nor Mejia had their eyes bandaged. Miramon, not addressing the soldiers, but the citizens assembled, said, "Mexicans! my judges have condemned me to death as a traitor to my country. I never was a traitor, and request you not to suffer this stain to be affixed to my memory, and still less' to my children. Viva Mexico! viva the Emperor!" The shots hit him well; he was dead on the spot.

Mejia only said, "Viva Mexico! viva the Emperor!" He lived after the firing, and required two more bullets to despatch him. All the three condemned were shot at the same moment.

After the death of the three had been confirmed by two surgeons, the bodies were wrapped in coarse sheets, and placed in common deal coffins, worth twenty reals a-piece, such as are used by the lowest class. That of the Emperor was much too short, and his feet protruded. The bodies of the two generals were delivered to their families, but that of the Emperor was reserved by the Republican Government for a low speculation, and was confided to the care of Colonel Don Miguel Palacios, the ferocious, squinting "hyena." He carried it between two detachments of infantry across the city, where its aspect caused everywhere great lamentation. An officer, revolver in hand, stepped up to a woman, and asked, in a harsh tone, "Why do you cry?" She answered, "I am weeping for my Emperor." Upon which he caught hold of her arm in order to arrest her, when she stabbed him with a knife, and escaped. The mourning in the city was general, and many persons, especially women, were arrested for expressing it in a too lively, passionate manner.

The behaviour of the inhabitants of Queré-taro cannot, indeed, be sufficiently praised and admired. For months they had suffered all the horrors of a siege. The shot of the enemy had destroyed their houses, and killed many of their friends and relations. They had suffered fear, sorrow, and hunger, and had to pay considerable contributions. But all this was not able to diminish their devotion and love for the Emperor, whom, indeed, they loved with enthusiasm. Though this is very explicable, it is not the less creditable to them.

The Mexicans are not used to a kind treatment from their robber-like generals, and here they saw a descendant of the Emperor of the Conquerors of Mexico walking daily amongst them, and showing sympathy and compassion with their sufferings, and an amiability which was in such striking contrast with the brutal behaviour of their own generals; a prince who shared all the dangers and deprivations of his subjects and soldiers, who had for every suffering a comforting, kind word, and who was an edifying example for every one. Now he was dead! He died with that greatness and serene calmness of soul which we admire so much in single instances in history, and the narrative of which edifies and touches the heart of all succeeding generations. The manner in which the noble Emperor died may justly be placed by the side of Socrates. The good people of Querétaro venerated him like a saint-martyr. Many dipped their handkerchiefs in his blood; others procured other relics, to the great vexation of his Republican murderers. Even on the "hyena" Palacios the greatness of the man made an impression, and he could not forbear saying, "He was a great soul!"

The body was placed on a table in the chapel of the Convent de los Capuchinos, and the colonel called in Dr. Basch, the servants, and a number of convalescent imprisoned officers, for the most part French, who were in the convent. Pointing to the body, he said to the latter, "Behold, that is the work of France!" These French officers used as a promenade a passage, through the windows of which they could look down into the chapel, and observe everything that was going on near the body of the Emperor, and I owe to them the following details:—

Soon afterwards, the chief physician of the Liberal army, Dr. Riva de Nera, accompanied by Dr. Licea, the betrayer of Miramon, and several other persons made their appearance, Dr. Basch was also permitted to be present, The body was then undressed, and prepared for embalming. The scenes which occurred here are in harmony with the lowness of mind of those present, and some details are so disgusting and revolting that I cannot speak of them.

That the doctors went to their work noisily, laughing, and smoking, may be pardonable, as they are used to such kind of work, and had not that veneration for the dead which we feel; but no one can excuse Dr. Licea, who said, when plunging his knife into the body of the dead prince, "What a delight it is for me to be able to wash my hands in the blood of an Emperor!"

Colonel Palacios tapped with his hand on the head of the body, and said, "Oh, you would place crowns upon your head? Now you will be satisfied now you have your crown;" and, pointing to two vessels in which the intestines of the Emperor were placed, he said, "Those ought to be given to the dogs."

The embalming lasted a whole week, and the heart of the Emperor was lying a whole day on one of the benches of the chapel. The embalmed body was then placed in a better coffin, and remained under guard in the chapel.

Colonel Palacios had appropriated the field-bed of the Emperor. When he had visitors he used to lay down on it, and say, "I am Emperor now! How do I look as an Emperor?"

When a Liberal officer expressed himself less brutally than the rest, Colonel Doria, secretary to Escobedo, said: "Pooh! what does it matter, one dog more or less?"

General Mirafuentes, who was later my fiscal, regretted, he said, the death of the two Mexicans; for the foreigner he did not care a straw.

During the last days before the execution of the Emperor, the question whether he ought to be shot was of course frequently discussed amongst the Liberal officers. One of them said that they had no right to shoot the Emperor, as the city had not been taken by storm, but bought together with the Emperor. "What does it matter," said one of the others, laughing, "chickens are bought also and killed."

The Querétaro paper ("La Sombra de Arteaga") of the 20th of June was printed on red paper, and contained only a short statement of the facts, without any comment.

If Escobedo had not wished the death of the Emperor, he might easily have prevented it, as Juarez would not have dared to act against the general to whom he owed so much. But Escobedo is not only bloodthirsty and a coward, but had also an interest in the removal of a rival, who appeared to him more dangerous than Juarez, Ortega, or Santa Anna. It was generally believed that the Emperor would not have been shot, if he had fallen into the hands of Porfirio Diaz instead of those of Escobedo.

The Emperor was about six feet high, and of a slender figure. His movements, his gait, and especially his greeting, were graceful and light. He had fair hair, not very thick, which he wore carefully parted in the middle. His beard was also fair and very long, and he nursed it with great care. He wore it parted in the middle, and his hand was very frequently occupied with its arrangement. The Emperor's complexion was pure and clear, and his eyes blue. His mouth had the unmistakeable stamp of the Austrian imperial house, the historical under lip, but not so much pronounced as to be disfiguring.

The Emperor was generally in citizen dress; but in Querétaro, where he stood at the head of his troops, he wore the uniform of a general of division.

When he promenaded, he had his hands behind his back, like a captain of a ship pacing the deck. Another naval habit was, of always carrying in his hand his perspective glass.

The expression of his face was almost always very kind and friendly: one could not look on him without loving him. His friendliness never showed itself in a familiar manner; even with his most intimate friends he always preserved his dignity. Notwithstanding this, he abandoned himself without restraint to his good humour, when in congenial company, and could be very witty and even sarcastic.

He was a very good listener, and fond of hearing the former adventures of the persons around him, whose faults he judged mildly, as he never supposed bad motives. Though he had seen and observed much during his travels, and was a man of very good sense, his heart was too noble and too pure for a profitable knowledge of the world. He had so little conception of wickedness and falsehood in others, that he never would believe in their existence in any man. He was very devoted and true to his friends, and thought more of them than of himself. He forgave easily, and that not only with his lips, but with his heart. Of all men I ever met with in life, the Emperor Maximilian was the noblest, best, and most amiable. Even his very faults were almost virtues; for instance, his kindness, which frequently bordered upon weakness. He could not bear to mortify a man, or harm him in any way, especially if he had done anything against him. He, for instance, did not think much of Baron Lago, the Austrian *chargé d'affaires*, and blamed the lukewarm and selfish faint-heartedness of that gentleman; still, he wrote to him before his death a few kind lines, that he might show them on his return to Vienna.

He was a great lover and connoisseur of the fine arts, and his feeling for fine forms went so far that it was painful for him to look on anything inharmonious or unsymmetrical. I suppose that was the reason why he was easily captivated by good-looking people, with pleasing, polished manners, as he always supposed that a fine human form must be animated by a fine soul. This feeling for harmony and order with the Emperor extended even to trifling things, which made him appear sometimes almost pedantic.

He liked to finish every business at once, and answered all questions with great patience, but it was disagreeable to him if he was reminded of the thing afterwards. Therefore he insisted that all his orders, even the most trifling, should be noted down at the very moment he gave them.

Those who would judge of the rich soul of the Emperor, should read his travels, which have been published in England and in different languages. They were, as I understand, published at the desire of his august mother, the Archduchess Sophia, who could not erect to her glorious son any better monument. Though written by the archduke when he was still very young, the whole man is revealed in its pages, and everyone who reads them will concur with me in thinking, what a pity this gifted prince was torn from the world where he might have done such extensive good!

To labour for the advancement of humanity and the progress of the world, was the highest ambition of the Emperor Maximilian. His ideas differed, however, so entirely from the old traditions of the Austrian court, that it was impossible for him to find suitable employment in his own country, which he ardently loved. The experienced tempter in Paris offered him a wide field for his aspirations, and the ambition of the descendant of Charles V. was by no means indifferent to the splendour of an imperial crown. The Emperor of the French had an easy game to play with an open chivalrous character like that of the young archduke. The favourite inclinations and desires of the young lofty-minded prince were skillfully worked upon, and Napoleon III. had not much trouble in captivating him by his proposition, which ought to have been examined with the more care, as it was made by a member of the Napoleonic family to one of the family of Austria. But in the noble unprejudiced soul of the archduke, traditional antipathies gave way to his objective admiration for the great statesman, which he expressed on several occasions, and whom he greatly overrated. Any scruples which he might have entertained were overbalanced by the prospect of a glorious and great sphere of usefulness. He who would benefit humanity must frequently dismiss antagonistic personal feelings and inclinations.

The philanthropic deceits of Napoleon were the snares in which the archduke, who longed for noble action, was the more easily caught, as his talents were rather a source of regret than of admiration in Vienna. His position there, indeed, was by no means agreeable, and created in him an ardent desire to escape from it as soon as was possible.

When misfortune came upon him, the mind of the Emperor of Mexico showed itself in its whole strength and moral dignity; and his last days and death are an edifying example for all ages.

The episode of the Mexican empire under Maximilian was too short, and did not leave any lasting effects in that unhappy country (where revolutions are its normal condition), so as to

take a prominent place in history by itself.
But this episode will exert an influence on the
history of Napoleon III. which gives it importance, as it forms the turning-point in the
career of the French emperor, on whom the
blood of the noble victim whom he permitted
to be sacrificed will certainly be revenged.
Though the necessities of policy compelled the
brother of Maximilian to join his hand with
that of Napoleon; still there is above us a
power that will not forget that by this hand
the blood of a noble and good man was spilt
at the far Cerro de la Campaña!

I frequently heard the Emperor called a
fanatical person and an adventurer; and I
cannot forbear saying a few words in reference
to this view of him.

There is in all history scarcely a single man
who ever accomplished great things who was
not called a fanatical person or adventurer
by his narrow-minded contemporaries. To a
mind which crawls always in the narrow atmosphere of his miserable self; and to a man for
whom the care of self seems to be the quintes-
sence of philosophical wisdom, to such petty
common-place people, every one who sacrifices
himself for the general good of humanity, re-
gardless of personal interest, must appear as a
weak-minded person, as an aspirant for a lunatic

asylum. For the " Philistine," even all philosophers and men of speculative sciences, of which the material good result is concealed from their weak eyes, are candidates for Bedlam.

With the epithet " adventurer," these " Philistines " are still more liberal. " Bleibe im Lande und naehre dich redlich "—stay at home and win your life honestly—is with them a favourite phrase. Whoever is urged beyond the narrow pale of his home, in search for a proper field for his active mind, is an adventurer, and only pardoned, though still always somewhat suspected, if he brings home tangible proofs of his good success.

" Whenever the time shall come, when poets shall bring the events of our days before the eyes of coming generations, there will not be missing amongst their most splendid figures that of the German Prince, who was carried by his high and noble desire beyond the ocean, and who found his tragical end in a fruitless struggle to confer the benefits of lawful order and true culture on a neglected people."*

* "The Imperial Tragedy in Mexico." Adolph Stern, Dresden. Publisher: M. Heinsius, 1867.

END OF VOL. I.

SD - #0024 - 010322 - C0 - 229/152/19 - PB - 9781331244394 - Gloss Lamination